S0-BYA-129

TORONTO MEDIEVAL LATIN TEXTS

The Canterbury Hymnal

Edited from

BRITISH LIBRARY MS. ADDITIONAL 37517

by

GERNOT R. WIELAND

Published for the
CENTRE FOR MEDIEVAL STUDIES

by the
PONTIFICAL INSTITUTE OF MEDIAEVAL STUDIES
Toronto

Canadian Cataloguing in Publication Data

Catholic Church.
  [Hymnary]
  The Canterbury hymnal

(Toronto medieval Latin texts, ISSN 0082-5050 ; 12)
Latin text, introd. and notes in English.
Bibliography: p.
ISBN 0-88844-462-1

1. Catholic Church — Hymns.   2. Hymns, Latin.
I. Wieland, Gernot R. (Gernot Rudolf), 1946-
II. Catholic Church. Psalter (Ms. British Library.
Additional 37517).   III. University of Toronto. Centre
for Medieval Studies.   IV. Pontifical Institute of
Mediaeval Studies.   V. Title.   VI. Series.

BV468.C38   245'.71   C82-094624-9

© 1982 by
The Pontifical Institute of Mediaeval Studies
59 Queen's Park Crescent East
Toronto, Ontario, Canada M5S 2C4

Printed and bound in Canada
by The Hunter Rose Company, 1982

PREFACE

The Toronto Medieval Latin Texts series is published for the Centre for Medieval Studies, University of Toronto, by the Pontifical Institute of Mediaeval Studies. The series is intended primarily to provide editions suitable for university courses and curricula, at a price within the range of most students' resources. Many Medieval Latin texts are available only in expensive scholarly editions equipped with full textual apparatus but with little or no annotation for the student; even more are out of print, available only in libraries; many interesting texts still remain unedited.

Editions in this series are usually based on one MS only, with a minimum of textual apparatus; emendations are normally made only where the text fails to make sense, not in order to restore the author's original version. Editors are required to select their MS with great care, choosing one that reflects a textual tradition as little removed from the original as possible, or one that is important for some other reason (such as a local variant of a text, or a widely influential version). Manuscript orthography and syntax are carefully preserved.

The Editorial Board is not merely supervisory: it is responsible for reviewing all proposals, for examining all specimens of editors' work, and for the final reading of all editions submitted for publication; it decides on all matters of editorial policy. Volumes are printed by photo-offset lithography, from camera-ready copy typed on an IBM Composer.

As General Editor, I would like to thank the Centre for Medieval Studies and its Directors, past and present, for their continuing support and encouragement at all stages in the development of the series.

A.G.R.

ACKNOWLEDGMENTS

Special thanks are due to Helmut Gneuss, who first suggested that these hymns be edited and then assisted me with invaluable advice. I also wish to express my gratitude to the editors of the series, and to the Keeper of Manuscripts of the British Library, who gave permission to publish this text.

G. R. W.

This book has been published with the help of a grant from the Canadian Federation for the Humanities, using funds provided by the Social Sciences and Humanities Research Council of Canada, whose support is acknowledged with thanks.

CONTENTS

INTRODUCTION

HISTORY AND DEFINITION OF HYMNS

St. Benedict's Rule

In any examination of the history of hymns a central place must be given to St. Benedict of Nursia, the founder of the Benedictine order. Benedict wrote no hymns himself, but in an important passage of his Rule he made the singing of hymns part of the daily office for the monks of his order:

> Ut ait propheta: *Septies in die laudem dixi tibi.* Qui septenarius sacratus numerus a nobis sic implebitur, si matutino, primae, tertiae, sextae, nonae, uesperae completoriique tempore nostrae seruitutis officia persolbamus, quia de his diurnis horis dixit: *Septies in die laudem dixi tibi.* Nam de nocturnis uigiliis idem ipse propheta ait: *Media nocte surgebam ad confitendum tibi.* Ergo his temporibus referamus laudes creatori nostro *super iudicia iustitiae* suae, id est matutinis, prima, tertia, sexta, nona, uespera, completorio; s<ed> et nocte surgamus ad confitendum ei.[1]

As the Benedictine order spread from Italy to the rest of Europe, it introduced the practice of singing hymns there as well.

---

1 *Benedicti regula,* ed. Rudolphus Hanslik, CSEL 75, 2nd ed. (Vienna 1977) pp. 70f. According to Dom Thomas Symons, ed., *Regularis concordia Anglicae nationis monachorum sanctimonialiumque* (London 1953) p. xliii, during the winter prayers were said as follows (summer horarium in brackets): Nocturns at 3 a.m. (2 a.m.), Lauds at 6 a.m. (3:30-4 a.m.), Prime at 6:45 a.m. (6 a.m.), Terce at 9 a.m. (8 a.m.), Sext at noon (11:30 a.m.), None at 1:30 p.m. (2:30 p.m.), Vespers at c. 4 p.m. (c. 5 p.m.), Compline at 6:15 p.m. (8 p.m.). The hymns form only part of the office. For a more detailed account of the daily office see Karl Young, *The Drama of the Medieval Church* (Oxford 1933) pp. 44-75. The daily office of a parish or cathedral church, which Young describes, may differ in detail from that of a monastery, but it has the same general outline.

Definition of the Term 'hymn'

Since the above passage refers to the entire office and not only
to hymns, a few words are necessary to indicate what is here
understood by the term 'hymn.' According to Isidore of Seville
hymns 'sunt continentes laudem Dei. Si ergo sit laus et non sit
Dei, non est hymnus: si sit et laus et Dei laus, et non cantetur,
non est hymnus. Si ergo et in laudem Dei dicitur et cantatur,
tunc est hymnus.'[2] Isidore's definition applies to hymns in
general. For this edition the term 'hymn' is narrowed down to
refer only to those songs in praise of God which formed part of
the daily office of the Benedictine monks, that is the metrical
compositions which were chanted at Prime, Terce, Sext, None,
Vespers, Compline, Nocturns, and Lauds. Not included in this
definition are antiphons and responsories, even though they can
be metrical, rhymed, and stanzaic and are part of the daily
office.[3]

The Origin of Hymn Singing in the Western Church

Psalm 118, which is quoted by Benedict, indicates that praise
of God, possibly in the form of hymns, made up part of the
daily routine for the devout even in Old Testament times. The
early church, especially in the East, may well have adopted this
custom from its beginning.[4] The introduction of this practice
into the Latin church, however, took place somewhat later. St.
Augustine describes the event in his *Confessiones:*

> Nimirum annus erat aut non multo amplius, cum
> Iustina Valentiniani regis pueri mater, hominem
> tuum Ambrosium persequeretur haeresis suae cau-
> sa, qua fuerat seducta ab Arrianis. excubabat pia

2 *Isidori Hispalensis episcopi etymologiarum sive originum libri XX,*
   ed. W.M. Lindsay (1911; repr. Oxford 1957) 6.19.17
3 For a similar definition of the term 'hymn' see also Helmut Gneuss,
   Hymnar und Hymnen im englischen Mittelalter, Buchreihe der Anglia
   12 (Tübingen 1968) p. 3.
4 See F.J.E. Raby, *A History of Christian-Latin Poetry from the Beginnings to the Close of the Middle Ages,* 2nd ed. (Oxford 1953) pp. 28-9.

> plebs in ecclesia, mori parata cum episcopo suo, servo
> tuo ... tunc hymni et psalmi ut canerentur secundum
> morem orientalium partium, ne populus maeroris
> taedio contabesceret, institutum est: ex illo in hodier-
> num retentum multis iam ac paene omnibus gregibus
> tuis et per cetera orbis imitantibus.[5]

The phrases 'secundum morem orientalium partium' and 'ex illo in hodiernum retentum' form the basis for our assumption that the Western church had not previously included hymns in the daily office, while it was common practice in the Eastern church.[6]

The hymns written by Ambrose gained rapid acceptance and were soon imitated by other writers. Such was Ambrose's authority that all hymns written in iambic dimeter came to be called 'Ambrosiani,' regardless of the actual author. Even though the origins of hymn singing were not monastic, various rules for monastic communities, such as those written by Caesarius and Aurelian,[7] and, as mentioned above, the Rule of St. Benedict, greatly contributed to the use of the hymns.

The Old Hymnal (= OH)

The evidence for the number and use of the hymns which these monastic rules afford is not very satisfactory, since often only the first line of a hymn is mentioned or only a vague term such as 'Ambrosianum' or 'hymnum eiusdem horae' given.[8] Nonetheless, using the monastic rules and several other sources, Gneuss

---

5   *St. Augustine's Confessions,* Loeb Classical Library (London 1912) II, 30 (= *Confessions* 9.7)
6   A.S. Walpole, *Early Latin Hymns* (Cambridge 1922; repr. Hildesheim 1966) p. 16, argues that 'hymns in themselves were by this time no novelty. But a new mode of singing them was then introduced.'
7   S. Caesarii Arelatensis episcopi, *Regula sanctarum virginum,* ed. G. Morin, Florilegium patristicum 34 (Bonn 1933); also his *Opera omnia,* ed. G. Morin (Maredsous 1937-42) II, 99-124. Aurelian, *Regula ad monachos,* PL 68.385-98 and *Regula ad virgines,* PL 68.399-406.
8   See, e.g., *Benedicti regula* 9.4 (p. 60), 12.4 (p. 65), 13.11 (p. 68), and 17.3 (p. 72).

has reconstructed the so-called Old Hymnal.[9] It 'dates back to the fifth century and was in general use until the eighth or ninth century.'[10] The OH contained approximately fifteen hymns, one for each canonical hour (Nocturns, Lauds, Prime, Terce, Sext, None, Vespers, Compline), one each for important feasts of the church (Christmas, Epiphany, Easter), and one each for some saints (Peter and Paul, John the Evangelist, several martyrs).

The OH in England

Evidence for the use of the OH in England is scanty. Bede's *De arte metrica* quotes parts of several hymns, there is one extant manuscript which contains three hymns, and there is a fifteenth-century description of a now lost late sixth/early seventh-century manuscript.[11] This is not sufficient to argue that the OH was definitely used in England. Nonetheless, such a scarcity of evidence is to be expected because of the loss of books caused by Viking raids and the dissolution of monasteries. Moreover, when the New Hymnal (= NH) was introduced into England around the middle of the tenth century the manuscripts containing the OH were obsolete, and many were probably re-used for other texts or even destroyed. Since three references to the OH in Anglo-Saxon times exist despite this great loss of manu-

9 Gneuss, pp. 10-40; for a list of the hymns of the OH see pp. 24-5.
10 Helmut Gneuss, 'Latin Hymns in Medieval England: Future Research,' in *Chaucer and Middle English Studies in Honour of Rossell Hope Robbins,* ed. Beryl Rowland (London 1974) p. 410.
11 Four of the seven hymns that Bede mentions also found their way into the NH (Hymns 2, 15, 31, and 80 of this ed.). The other three ('Rex aeterne domine,' 'Iam surgit hora tertia,' 'Intende qui regis Israel') are part of the OH, but do not appear in the MS of this ed. The extant MS is BL Cotton Vespasian A I; it has been edited by Sherman M. Kuhn under the title *The Vespasian Psalter* (Ann Arbor 1965). Its three hymns are 'Splendor paternae gloriae' (Hymn 15 of this ed.), 'Deus creator omnium' (Hymn 31), and 'Rex aeterne Domine.' The description of the lost MS is found in Thomas of Elmham, *Historia monasterii S. Augustini Cantuariensis,* ed. Ch. Hardwick, Rolls Series 8 (London 1858) p. 97f.

scripts, it seems very likely that the OH was in fact known and used in England.

The New Hymnal (= NH)

During the ninth century the so-called New Hymnal was created on the continent.[12] The major characteristic which distinguishes it from the OH is the greater number of hymns. The earliest continental manuscript containing the NH has 38 hymns,[13] as opposed to the approximately 15 hymns for the OH, and the earliest English manuscript (BL MS. Add. 37517, designated as *B*) contains 100 hymns.[14] A desire for greater diversification probably lies at the root of the NH. The OH consisted primarily of the *Ordinarium de tempore;*[15] only five hymns were set aside for the *Proprium de tempore et proprium sanctorum*[16] and the *Commune sanctorum.*[17] This means that the monks chanted practically the same hymns day in, day out. The NH as manifested in the earliest English manuscript, on the other hand, pro-

12 See Gneuss, pp. 55-74. This introduction intentionally omits mention of the so-called Frankish Hymnal (Gneuss, 'Latin Hymns,' p. 409f.), since there is no evidence that it was ever used in England.

13 The original MS containing this hymnal has been separated into two parts which can now be found in St. Paul in Kärnten, Stiftsbibliothek, MS. 25.2.31b and in Karlsruhe, Landesbibliothek, Augiensis CXCV.

14 In counting the hymns I follow the rubrication of the scribe and ignore the separation of one hymn into several parts. Hymns 52, 56, 58, 65, and 69 appear as only one hymn each in the MS. In actual use Hymns 52, 56, and 58 were probably separated into two parts and 65 and 69 into three parts, and each of these parts was chanted at a different hour. Taking the divisions into account B contains 107 hymns altogether.

15 The *Ordinarium de tempore* contains a body of hymns that were to be chanted on ordinary weekdays and Sundays, i.e. on any day that was not a feastday.

16 The *Proprium de tempore et proprium sanctorum* contains a body of hymns that were to be chanted on feastdays of the church (e.g. Christmas, Easter), on feastdays of saints, and during special seasons (e.g. Advent or Lent).

17 The *Commune sanctorum* contains a body of hymns that were to be chanted on feastdays of saints for whom no special hymns had been

vides sixty-eight hymns for the *Proprium de tempore et proprium sanctorum* and the *Commune sanctorum.* Even the *Ordinarium de tempore* is more diversified, since it offers different Nocturns, Lauds, and Vespers for every day of the week (Terce, Sext, and None remain the same on every day of the week throughout the year, except for Lent). The daily repetition of the same body of hymns is avoided in the NH.

The NH in England

We do not know at what period the NH came from the continent to England. The earliest manuscript containing it is dated approximately 970, but it may have been on the island before that. Doubtless the Benedictine Reform, begun under Dunstan around 940, when he became abbot of Glastonbury, and under the two bishops Oswald and Æthelwold, was responsible for a wide dissemination of the NH. Unfortunately, extant manuscripts proving such a dissemination prior to 970 are missing; and the *Regularis concordia,* which prescribes the use of certain hymns of the NH,[18] was written at about the same time as the earliest extant manuscript. We can therefore only suggest that in all likelihood the efforts of the reformers brought the NH into England as early as 940, but there is no substantial proof

composed. Hymns 81-90 seem to be misplaced in the *Commune sanctorum,* since they honour specific saints, all of them apostles, and should therefore be included in the *Proprium sanctorum.* This apparent irregularity can be explained easily: only the first stanza differs with each hymn, while stanzas 2-5 of Hymn 81 are common to all of them. These latter stanzas, which the scribe wrote only once, are therefore responsible for the inclusion of Hymns 81-90 in the *Commune sanctorum.*

18 The following hymns which are mentioned in the *Regularis concordia* occur only in the NH: 'O lux beata' (Hymn 32, mentioned on p. 25 in the *Regularis conc.*), 'Primo dierum' (Hymn 1 — p. 25), 'Nocte surgentes' (Hymn 3 — p. 58), 'Ecce iam noctis' (Hymn 4 — p. 58). Moreover, references to 'the usual ferial hymns' (p. 25) and to hymns of the season for Advent, Lent, and Passiontide (p. 25) clearly indicate that the *Regularis conc.* drew on the NH since the OH did not have different hymns for the days of the week or for various seasons.

for this suggestion.

As Gneuss has shown, there are two types of the NH in England during the tenth and eleventh centuries.[19] He divides these into the Winchester group (= Wi) and the Canterbury group (= Ca). Wi has fewer hymns than Ca, and a number of hymns which are common to both are used differently. Wi is not an earlier form of Ca, nor is Ca an earlier form of Wi. Gneuss suggests that the different hymnals may have come from different continental monasteries: Wi probably from Fleury, Ca possibly from Ghent.

Wi does not need to be described in detail here, but more detail is necessary on Ca. Three manuscripts containing it are still extant: *B,* about which more later; *D* (Durham Cathedral MS. B III 32, first half of the eleventh century); and *V* (BL MS. Cotton Vespasian D XII, middle of the eleventh century).[20] Two of these manuscripts (*B* and *D*) stem from Canterbury, and the third (*V*) most likely comes from there as well. *D* and *V,* the two more recent manuscripts, each have approximately twenty hymns more than *B,* including hymns for local saints such as Dunstan, Augustine of Canterbury, and Cuthbert.[21] Because of its earlier date and because of the smaller number of hymns, *B* is the earliest extant representative of Ca.

19 Gneuss, pp. 69-74

20 MSS *D* and *V* are described in greater detail in N.R. Ker, *Catalogue of Manuscripts containing Anglo-Saxon* (Oxford 1957) under nos. 107A and 208, and in Gneuss, pp. 85-90 and 98-101.

21 Hymns in honour of St. Cuthbert occur in *D* on fol. 20r, in *V* on fol. 57v; in honour of St. Dunstan in *D* on fol. 28v, in *V* on fol. 120v; in honour of St. Augustine of Canterbury in *D* on fols. 29r, 29v, and 30r, but not at all in *V*.

THE BOSWORTH PSALTER

Contents

We can now turn to BL MS. Add. 37517, which is also known as the Bosworth Psalter (= *B*). The manuscript was written in the second half of the tenth century. In its original form it consisted of: a Roman Psalter on folios 4r-95r, the so-called Psalm 151 on folio 95v,[22] canticles on folios 96r-104r, hymns on folios 105r-128r, and monastic canticles on folios 129r-135r. This list shows that in its earliest form the Bosworth Psalter contained many important texts of the Benedictine Office. In later times different scribes added: a calendar on folios 2r-3r (tenth/eleventh century), incipits of prayers on folio 64r (twelfth century), a litany on folios 104r-104v (tenth/eleventh century), and prayers and texts of the Mass on folios 135v-139v (tenth/eleventh century). Folios 1r and 3v are blank, and 128v contains an illustration of Christ.[23]

Date

The manuscript is generally considered to have been composed in the second half of the tenth century, 'probably at a date nearer to the middle of the century than to the end' according to Gasquet and Bishop,[24] in 'the last quarter of the tenth century' according to Korhammer.[25] This date is suggested primarily by the palaeographical features of the manuscript. Some negative evidence has been taken into account as well: unlike

22 The apocryphal, so-called Psalm 151 was supposedly written by David after he had defeated Goliath. For a text see Kuhn, *Vespasian Psalter*, p. 146.

23 For more detailed descriptions of the entire MS see Abbot Gasquet and Edmund Bishop, *The Bosworth Psalter* (London 1908); Ker, no. 129; Minnie Cate Morrell, *A Manual of Old English Biblical Materials* (Knoxville 1965) pp. 126-30; and no. 22 in E. Temple, *Anglo-Saxon Manuscripts 900-1066* (London 1976).

24 Gasquet and Bishop, p. 127

25 P.M. Korhammer, 'The Origin of the Bosworth Psalter,' *ASE* 2 (1973) 173.

other Canterbury hymnals, such as those contained in *V* or *D, B* does not contain any hymn in honour of St. Dunstan and is therefore supposed to have been written before that saint's death on May 19, 988. Because of its contents there can be no doubt that the manuscript is closely connected with the Benedictine Reform. *B,* as was mentioned above, originates from Canterbury: therefore a possible *terminus a quo* for the manuscript's composition is A.D. 959, the year in which Dunstan, the leader of the Benedictine Reform movement, became archbishop of Canterbury. Neither Korhammer's supposition that the last quarter of the tenth century is the date of *B*'s composition, nor Gasquet and Bishop's conjecture of an earlier date, can be disproved. *B* may have been written at any time between approximately 960 and 990.

Provenance

Korhammer convincingly eliminates St. Augustine's monastery as a possible place of provenance.[26] In all likelihood *B* was written at Christ Church, Canterbury. The Psalter may even have been in St. Dunstan's possession: he was archbishop of Christ Church at the time of its composition, he was most interested in bringing about the Benedictine Reform, and he was one of the few people of the time who could afford a manuscript 'so notable in its art and execution.'[27]

---

26 Korhammer, p. 178. A possible objection to Korhammer's argument is that Christ Church became a Benedictine cathedral priory only in A.D. 997, and that the Benedictine Office would not have been used there before that date. David Knowles, *The Monastic Order in England: A History of its Development from the Times of St. Dunstan to the Fourth Lateran Council 940-1216,* 2nd ed. (Cambridge 1963), cautiously suggests that 'indications are not wanting that some monks, at least, were at Christ Church in [Dunstan's] day' (p. 50) and 'that Dunstan began gradually to introduce monks' (p. 697). If his opinion is correct, then at least one part of the clergy of Christ Church followed the Rule and required a text such as *B* provides.

27 Gasquet and Bishop, p. 126

THE HYMNAL IN THE BOSWORTH PSALTER

Description

The hymns in *B* are contained on folios 105r-128r. They are arranged in two columns per page, twenty-five lines per column, except folios 120v, 121r and v, and 122r and v, which contain twenty-four lines per page. All the hymns were written in the same (insular) hand; only on folio 108 ra 21 did a later (Carolingian) hand add a line which had originally been omitted. The hymnal is not glossed, either in Latin or in Old English, though other sections of *B* contain glosses.[28]

Accent marks occur on thirty-eight words; the colour of the ink indicates that the scribe who wrote the text also inserted the accent marks. All of them are included in this edition. They were most likely inserted to facilitate the reading aloud of the text and are not intended as metrical aids.

Metrics

This introduction is not the place to enter into a detailed examination of the metres of the hymns in *B:* the reader is referred to the literature listed on pages 21-2.[29] The discussion here will deal primarily with the manner in which the scribe indicated his knowledge of the various metres.

28 The OE glosses in the Psalter are published in Uno Lindelöf, 'Die altenglischen Glossen im Bosworth-Psalter,' *Mémoires de la Société néophilologique à Helsingfors* 5 (1909) 139-200.

29 The metres of the hymns in *B* are both quantitative, i.e. based on the length of syllables, and rhythmic, i.e. based on the natural stress on words. The metrical schemes below are simplified somewhat in that both systems are conflated. The following metres occur in the hymns: *sapphic stanza:* $\stackrel{\prime}{-}\cup-\stackrel{\prime}{-}-//\cup\cup\stackrel{\prime}{-}\cup\stackrel{\prime}{-}\cup$ for the first three lines and $\stackrel{\prime}{-}\cup\cup\stackrel{\prime}{-}\cup$ for the fourth line (Hymns 3-4, 43, 55, 69, 71, 74, 77, 95, and 98-9).
catalectic iambic trimeter: $\cup\stackrel{\prime}{-}\cup\stackrel{\prime}{-}\cup\stackrel{\prime}{-}\cup$ (Hymn 13).
asclepiad: $---\cup\cup-//\stackrel{\prime}{-}\cup\cup\stackrel{\prime}{-}\cup$ or $---\cup\cup-//\stackrel{\prime}{-}\cup\cup\stackrel{\prime}{-}\cup\underset{\cup}{}$ (the imitation of this scheme in rhythmic verse has several variants for the first six syllables; see Norberg, pp. 98ff. The asclepiad is found in

Most of the hymns in *B* are composed in the iambic dimeter.
The scribe showed an awareness of this metre by giving one line
to each verse. Only occasionally at the beginning of a hymn,
when he used ornate capitals, did he use two or three lines for
one verse. He allowed, for instance, two and a half lines for the
first, and one and a half lines for the second verse of Hymn 1:

> PRI
> MO DIERVM
> omnium. quo mundus
> extat conditus.
> uel quo resurgens conditor
> nos morte uicta liberet.

He nevertheless indicated the end of the verse by means of a
punctum, as here after *omnium* and *conditus*. [30]

The eight syllables of the iambic dimeter easily fit into one
line of a column. That space becomes too cramped, however,
for verses with eleven (Hymns 3 and 4, for example), twelve
(Hymns 81-90), or even fifteen syllables, and the scribe must
use more than one line per verse. The first stanza of Hymn 77
(a sapphic stanza), for instance, appears in the manuscript as
follows:

> Omnium Christe. pariter
> tuorum. festa sanctorum.
> colimus precantes. hos tibi

the first two lines of Hymn 36, in Hymns 45 and 46, and in the
first three lines of 94).

dactylic hexameter: – ∪∪ – ∪∪ – ∪∪ – ∪∪ – ∪∪ – ∪ (Hymn 40).

trochaic trimeter: –́∪ –́∪ –́∪ (Hymn 57).

trochaic tetrameter: alternating between –́∪ –́∪ –́∪ –́∪ for the uneven
lines and –́∪ –́∪ –́∪ –́ for the even lines (Hymns 44 and 73).

iambic trimeter: ∪–́∪–́∪// –́∪–́∪–́∪–́ (Hymns 70 and 81-90).

iambic dimeter: ∪–́∪–́∪–́∪–́ (all other hymns).

Note that many of the long syllables can be replaced by two short
ones, and two short ones by one long one, and that in some places a
spondee can replace the trochee or the iamb.

30 The scribe used the punctum almost exclusively. Only very occasionally do we find other punctuation marks such as :-- on fol. 115rb9
or ; on fol. 116va7.

> qui iam. meruere iungi.
> nostra tueri

As with Hymn 1 above, the scribe used a punctum to indicate the end of a verse (here after *tuorum, precantes,* and *iungi*); in addition he marked the place of the caesura with a punctum.

Throughout the hymnal the beginning of each stanza is indicated by a capital letter. More ornate and larger capitals point out the beginning of each new hymn.

Rhyme and abecedarii

Aside from the metre two points concerning the mechanics of the poetry need to be mentioned here. (1) Many hymns have rhyming lines. The use of rhyme is frequent, but by no means consistent. Not taking into account the doxologies we find that only Hymns 20, 34, and 47 are rhymed consistently throughout. (2) This collection of hymns contains two abecedarii, that is, poems in which the first letter of every line or stanza is determined by alphabetical sequence. This alphabetical order is evident in the first letters of every line of Hymn 27, and in the first letters of every stanza of Hymns 41 and 42, which together form one poem. The early Christian poets such as Sedulius (the author of 41 and 42) may have used this manner of composition in imitation of Psalm 118.

Authors

The authors of liturgical texts are usually unknown; the writers of many of these hymns are no exception. Despite painstaking efforts of scholars, seventy-five of the hundred hymns of this edition are still anonymous and likely to remain so. Of the remaining twenty-five, thirteen can be attributed to an author with some degree of certainty, twelve with some degree of doubt. In chronological order the authors are: Ambrose (c. 340-397), Prudentius (c. 348-407), Sedulius (first half of the fifth century), Venantius Fortunatus (c. 540-600), Bede (c. 673-735), Paulus Diaconus (c. 720-800), Alcuin (c. 735-804), and Rabanus Maurus (c. 780-856). The following is a list of the hymns attributed to these writers and the degree of certainty:

Author	Certainly	Possibly
Ambrose	2, 15, 31, 80, 100	6, 7, 8
Prudentius	13, 18, 21, 24	
Sedulius	41, 42	
Venantius F.	58	56
Bede	63	
Paulus D.		69
Alcuin		3, 4
Rabanus M.		36, 43, 73, 74, 94

Hymns 1, 14, 16-17, 19-20, 22-3, 25-30, 32, 52, 54, and 67
have at times been attributed either to Gregory the Great or to
Ambrose; Hymn 66 was once attributed to Rabanus Maurus
and Hymn 70 to a Sicilian lady by the name of Elpis. Since
there is no substantial evidence for any of these attributions,
according to Szöverffy or Walpole (see Bibliography) or sometimes both, all these hymns must be considered as the compositions of anonymous writers.

Language

This collection contains hymns composed over the span of five
centuries, as the above list shows. The anonymous hymns come
from approximately the same period. Often the only evidence
for dating the anonymous hymns is the manuscript in which they
first appear. (Occasionally there is some other evidence: the
hymns of the OH, for instance, which are mentioned in the rules
of Caesarius and Aurelian, have a *terminus ante quem* in the
dates of the rules' composition.) The language of the fourth-
century poets is still very strongly influenced by classical Latin,
but by the ninth century Medieval Latin has taken on strong
characteristics of its own. Because of the time span and also the
regional diversity involved in the composition of the hymns, it
is impossible to speak of the language of the hymns as though
it were a uniform phenomenon. Certain semantic features, to be
sure, separate it from classical Latin. If any general rule can be

established, perhaps it is this: the Christian writers included
more Latinized Greek words such as *plasmator* (28.1), *agie*
(33.21), *cyrographo* (47.12), *plasmatis* (52.26), *gastrimargiae*
(53.7), *barathro* (60.22), *crismatis* (63.10), *protoplastis* (64.16),
paraclytus (65.33), and *zabulum* (73.12) in their vocabulary
than classical writers would have done.[31] This is almost to be
expected, since the language of the liturgy during the first few
centuries of the Latin church was Greek, and the early Chris-
tians took over a large number of Greek words as loanwords;
these then became an integral part of the Christian dialect.[32]
The few Hebrew words which occur in these hymns, such as
pascha (60.13), *alleluia* (45.1), and *amen* (at the end of all doxologies) separate the Christian from the classical Latin authors
as well.

The language of the hymns — no matter when they were
composed — is, of course, heavily influenced by that of the
Bible. The poets of the hymns sometimes echo entire phrases
(for example, 35.8-9 'ut tollat omne noxium./E sursum agnus
mittitur' = John 1:29 'Ecce agnus Dei, ecce qui tollit peccatum
mundi'; or 54.10-11 'amicus intimus/sponsi Iohannes claruit'
= John 3:29 'amicus autem sponsi, qui stat ...'). At other times
they merely allude to events in the Old or the New Testament,
or paraphrase passages from them (for example, the first eight
or twelve lines of Hymns 16, 19, 22, 25, and 28 allude to and
paraphrase Genesis 1:6-31). The approximately eighty refer-

31 Because of the date of many of the hymns the grecisms could possibly have been introduced by the so-called 'hermeneutic' writers
   (see Michael Lapidge, 'The Hermeneutic Style in Tenth-Century
   Anglo-Latin Literature,' *ASE* 4 [1975] 67-111). There are two ob-
   jections to such an assumption: (1) the grecisms in the hymns are
   rare and occur in isolation, while typically 'hermeneutic' passages
   usually abound in them; (2) the use of grecisms forms only one part
   of the 'hermeneutic' style. The other is a predilection for 'long,
   tortuously convoluted periods' (Lapidge, p. 69 — but in a different
   context). Since this second element is missing in the hymns, the
   grecisms most likely do not stem from a 'hermeneutic' stylist.
32 Such common words as *baptismum, epiphania, Pentecoste,* and even
   ecclesia are all of Greek origin.

ences to the Old and New Testaments which are provided in the notes are intended to familiarize the reader with the major events to which the poets are alluding, and to clarify the more obscure echoes. They also indicate the extent to which the poets depended on the Bible as their source of material and of language.

Few other generalizations can be put beside the two mentioned above. Pages 402-9 of Walpole's edition contain a very brief examination of the language of the hymns, but, as the editor notes, it does not (and probably cannot) attain any completeness. The reader's best introduction to the language of the hymns is any work dealing with the language of any particular author (if he is known), or such general works as Mohrmann's *Etudes sur le latin des chrétiens* (see bibliography).

Neums

The reader of the hymns may lose sight of the fact that they consist not only of metrical language but also of music. Isidore's definition (see page 2) demands that a poem in praise of God be chanted in order to qualify as a hymn. *B* contains only very scant information as to the tunes to which these hymns were sung. Musical notations, the so-called neums, appear on folios 106 va 7-14 (Hymn 9.1-8), 126 vb 1-4 (Hymn 95.1-4), and 126 vb 22-4 and 127 ra 1 (Hymn 96.1-4). Neums of the type found on these folios are called 'staffless, oratorical, cheironomic (Greek for hand sign), or in *campo aperto*.'[33] They do not provide exact melodies but rather 'served only as a guide for singers who knew the melodies more or less by heart, or for the choir leader who may have interpreted them to the singers by appropriate movements of the hand.'[34]

Rubrics

All but three hymns (1, 95, and 98) are prefaced by rubrics which prescribe at which canonical hour and what day of the

33 Willi Apel, *Gregorian Chant* (London 1958) p. 118
34 Apel, p. 118

year they are to be chanted. Two rubrics – for Hymns 24 and
56 – are incorrect: despite its beginning 'Lux ecce surgit aurea'
Hymn 24 is assigned to Nocturns instead of Lauds, and Hymn
56 is prescribed for Candlemas (February 2) rather than Annunciation (March 25). There are three reasons why the latter rubric
cannot be correct: (1) the scribe has already assigned Hymn 43
to Candlemas; (2) if Hymn 56 were indeed intended for Candlemas it would be misplaced, since the *Proprium de tempore et
proprium sanctorum* is structured in chronological order; (3)
the other Ca manuscripts, *V* on folio 61r and *D* on folio 22r,
assign Hymn 56 to Annunciation.

While all the other rubrics are correct, many give incomplete
information. They make, for instance, no distinction between
summer and winter hymns (see Hymns 2 and 4, or 10/11 and
12/13). Hymn 50 is assigned for Vespers daily during Lent.
Hymns 51 through 54 are all introduced by the rubric *ITEM
ALIUS YMNUS*.[35] This suggests that the monastic community
had at its disposal five hymns for Vespers daily during Lent,
but does not reveal whether they should be used successively on
Mondays, Tuesdays, Wednesdays, etc. or the first hymn should
be sung in the first week, the second in the second, etc., or if
each one can arbitrarily be chosen for any day. The rubric is
too vague to allow a definite conclusion as to the hymns' use.
Because of the unsatisfactory nature of many of these rubrics
a brief statement on use introduces each hymn printed in this
edition.

Doxologies

Hymns usually end in what is called a doxology. Originally this
was a verse in praise of God, as shown by the etymology of the
word, which derives from Greek $\delta\acute{o}\xi\alpha$ (= Latin *gloria*). Typical
doxologies are: 'Deo patri sit gloria' (Hymn 2), 'Laus, honor,
uirtus, gloria' (33), 'Gloria tibi, domine' (37), and 'Gloria tibi,

---

35 The scribe is not consistent in his orthography of *hymnus*. In the
rubrics he uses *hymnus* 48 times and *ymnus* 25 times.

trinitas' (47). Side by side with these appear formulae that
make a request of God: 'Presta, pater piissime' (Hymn 1),
'Prestet hoc nobis deitas beata' (3), 'Presta, pater omnipotens'
(10), 'Presta, beata trinitas' (51), etc. Both types of doxology
share an address to all three persons of the Trinity, whereby
particular care is taken not to subordinate any of the divine
persons to the others. The doxology of Hymn 1, for instance,
stresses that the Father, the Son, and the Holy Ghost are *compar,* and the doxology of Hymn 2 co-ordinates the three divine
persons with the co-ordinating conjunctions *-que* and *cum.* In
the fourth century formulae stressing the equality of the Trinity
were intended as polemical statements against Arianism, a heresy
that denied that God the Father and Christ are of the same substance and hence equally divine. In later centuries these doxologies became statements of the singers' belief (see also the
Creed in the Appendix).

The doxologies are so formulaic that any one can be attached
to several hymns, provided both hymn and doxology are composed in the same metre. The doxology for Hymn 2 (written in
iambic dimeter), for instance, appears at the end of Hymns 5,
11-13, 15, 18, 21, 24, 27, 30, 32, 58, 66, 78-9, 91, 93, and 100.

The scribe often provides only the first line of the doxology.
Footnotes refer the reader to the hymn that gives the complete text.

THIS EDITION OF THE HYMNAL

Choice of Manuscript

This edition is the first that is based entirely on *B.* Such an edition is desirable because of the nature of both the manuscript
and previous editions of the hymns.

As outlined above, the hymnal in this manuscript is the oldest complete extant English example of the NH.[36] As such it

---

36 Equally old, or even a bit older, is Durham Cathedral MS. A.IV.19.
   This MS, however, contains only twelve hymns or parts of hymns.

constitutes an early form of the hymnals found in manuscripts
V and *D*. Because of its age it must be considered as one of the
most important manuscripts documenting the revival of Benedictine monasticism in Anglo-Saxon England. If the manuscript
was, as has been assumed, expressly written for Dunstan, the
leader of the reform movement, its historical value increases.
Gasquet and Bishop's claim, moreover, that 'the state of the
MS. makes it certain that it was regularly used'[37] is an indica-
tion that it actually influenced the monks of Christ Church in
Canterbury. Finally, the text of the manuscript is very reliable,
as the scarcity of entries in the Textual Notes (see pages 132-3)
and the nature of the variants show.

Even though all the hymns of *B* have been previously published, none of the earlier editions can be considered fully
satisfactory. The *Analecta Hymnica* (= *AH*),[38] which is usually
regarded as the most authoritative text, contains all the hymns
of this edition: eighty-seven are contained in volumes 50 and
51, and the remaining thirteen spread out over volumes 1, 11,
14, 19, 23, and 27.[39] The NH, as represented in *B*, is thus not
conveniently accessible in *AH*. Moreover, the readings of *B* are
not used in *AH* despite the obvious importance of this manuscript as the oldest English representative of the NH.

The *Anglo-Saxon Hymnarium*[40] contains all but two hymns
of this edition, grouped in almost the same order as the hymns
of *B*;[41] it also contains interlinear Anglo-Saxon glosses. But it

37 Gasquet and Bishop, p. 126
38 *Analecta hymnica medii aevi*, ed. Clemens Blume and Guido M.
   Dreves, 55 vols. (Leipzig 1886-1922; repr. New York 1961).
39 Some hymns occur in several vols. Hymn 55, e.g., occurs in *AH* 2.40
   and 14.63. For the enumeration I have taken only one vol. into
   account. Only *AH* 50 and 51 are critical editions.
40 *The Latin Hymns of the Anglo-Saxon Church*, ed. J. Stevenson, Surtees Society 23 (Durham 1851). The term *Anglo-Saxon Hymnarium*
   occurs on p. 1 and is used throughout the book in place of a title.
41 Gasquet claims on p. 12 that 'the only hymn occurring in Bosworth
   and not in the Surtees volume is ... "Summe confessor sacer et sacerdos" ' (Hymn 98 of this ed.). In fact there are two hymns that are
   not contained in the Surtees vol.: Hymns 98 and 13 of this ed.

is not readily available because of its age, contains numerous
errors, and provides no commentary on individual hymns.

A very useful edition, which also takes into account the
readings of *B,* is Walpole's *Early Latin Hymns.* The hymns there
are not arranged in the order of the manuscripts, but appear
first under the names of the authors (when known) and then
under the headings 'Earlier Hymnal' and 'Later Hymnal.' Since
Walpole publishes only sixty-three of the hundred hymns of *B,*
however, his book cannot be considered a complete edition of
the NH.

The present edition complements previous editions by giving
a complete text of the NH, using the readings of a most important manuscript which has hitherto been neglected.

Editorial Practice

In this edition I have attempted to remain as close to the text
of *B* as possible. Occasionally an emendation was necessary,
either to make grammatical sense of a sentence or to restore the
metre of a line. Wherever possible I have supplied emendations
from *V* and *D,* since these manuscripts are also of the Ca type
and are relatively close in time to *B.* When *V* and *D* share a cor-
rupt text with *B,* or when *V*'s and *D*'s texts contain a mistake
different from that of *B,* or when *V* and *D* do not contain the
hymn of *B* that requires an emendation, I have used the text of
Walpole or *AH.* Only five such emendations were necessary (see
Textual Notes, pages 132-3). In some twenty instances where
Walpole gives a grammatically easier or metrically smoother
text than *B,* I have not emended *B,* but added Walpole's version
in a footnote.[42]

The orthography of the manuscript is reproduced faithfully.

42 In the notes I use the somewhat awkward term 'orig.' instead of Wal.
   This is because the designation Wal. does not clearly show whether we
   are dealing with a conjecture by this editor or with the evidence of
   the majority of MSS. The term 'orig.' refers to the reading of the
   majority of MSS; it is placed in quotation marks because the text is
   only presumably that of the original author.

Thus, when an *e* stands for an *ae,* or an *ę* or *æ* for an *e,* they have not been changed. Throughout, the manuscript reading *u* has been retained for both the vowel and the consonant, and *V* and *U* have been reproduced regardless whether they indicate the vowel or the consonant.

The punctuation has been modernized. On the scribe's use of punctuation see pages 11 and 12.

All proper names have been capitalized, even though they are not capitalized in the manuscript. Occasional intrusive capitals, such as in the words *confundereNT* (folio 108 ra15), *comprimaNT* (folio 108 rb 3), or *SpleNdor* (folio 107 vb 5), have not been reproduced.

One virgule (/) indicates the end of a column, two virgules (//) the end of a manuscript page.

All scribal abbreviations have been expanded silently. Words in < ... > have been added editorially; words in [...] are to be deleted. Other emendations are not signalled in the text, but the original readings of B are given in the Textual Notes.

Each hymn is introduced by brief statements indicating *use, author,* and relevant *literature.* The *author* category is omitted if the composer of a hymn is not known. The *literature* category includes abbreviated references to *AH,* Stevenson, Walpole, Gneuss, and Szöverffy (see Bibliography). The first three are the previous editions which this volume complements; references to Gneuss are included because his book contains an *Expositio hymnorum,* a Latin prose paraphrase of the hymns which is of as much value to modern students as it was to their Anglo-Saxon predecessors. References are also given to Szöverffy because his is one of the most recent scholarly efforts to deal comprehensively with hymns.

BIBLIOGRAPHY

Analecta hymnica medii aevi, ed. Clemens Blume and Guido M. Dreves, 55 vols. (Leipzig 1886-1922; repr. New York 1961) [cited as *AH*]

Apel, Willi. *Gregorian Chant* (London 1958)

Beare, William. *Latin Verse and European Song: A Study in Accent and Rhythm* (London 1957)

Benedicti regula, ed. Rudolphus Hanslik, CSEL 75, 2nd ed. (Vienna 1977)

Gasquet, A. and Edmund Bishop. *The Bosworth Psalter* (London 1908)

Gneuss, Helmut. *Hymnar und Hymnen im englischen Mittelalter,* Buchreihe der Anglia 12 (Tübingen 1968) [cited as Gneuss]
——————. 'Latin Hymns in Medieval England: Future Research,' in *Chaucer and Middle English Studies in Honour of Rossell Hope Robbins,* ed. Beryl Rowland (London 1974) pp. 407-24 [cited as Gneuss, 'Latin Hymns']

Klopsch, Paul. *Einführung in die mittellateinische Verslehre* (Darmstadt 1972)

Korhammer, P.M. 'The Origin of the Bosworth Psalter,' *ASE* 2 (1973) 173-87

Manitius, Max. *Geschichte der lateinischen Literatur des Mittelalters. Erster Band: Von Justinian bis zur Mitte des zehnten Jahrhunderts* (Munich 1911)

Mohrman, Christine. *Etudes sur le latin des chrétiens,* 3 vols. (Rome 1961-5)

Morrell, Minnie Cate. *A Manual of Old English Biblical Materials* (Knoxville 1965)

Norberg, Dag. *Introduction à l'étude de la versification latine médiévale,* Acta universitatis Stockholmiensis, Studia Latina Stockholmiensia 5 (Stockholm 1958)

Raby, F.J.E. *A History of Christian-Latin Poetry from the Beginning to the Close of the Middle Ages,* 2nd ed. (Oxford 1953)

Stevenson, J., ed. *The Latin Hymns of the Anglo-Saxon Church,*

Surtees Society 23 (Durham 1851) [cited as Stev.]

Symons, Dom Thomas, ed. and trans. *Regularis concordia Anglicae nationis monachorum sanctimonialiumque* (London 1953)

Szöverffy, Josef. *Die Annalen der lateinischen Hymnendichtung: Ein Handbuch. I, Die lateinischen Hymnen bis zum Ende des 11. Jahrhunderts* (Berlin 1964) [cited as Szov.]

Temple, E. *Anglo-Saxon Manuscripts 900-1066* (London 1976)

Wagner, Peter. *Einführung in die gregorianischen Melodien. Zweiter Teil: Neumenkunde* (Leipzig 1912; repr. Hildesheim 1962)

Walpole, A.S. *Early Latin Hymns* (Cambridge 1922; repr. Hildesheim 1966) [cited as Wal.]

Abbreviations

In addition to those listed above, the following abbreviations are used in this volume:

ASE	*Anglo-Saxon England*
B	Bosworth Psalter = BL MS. Add. 37517
Ca	Canterbury group
CCSL	Corpus Christianorum, series Latina
CSEL	Corpus scriptorum ecclesiasticorum Latinorum
D	Durham Cathedral MS. B III 32
Etymologiae	*Isidori Hispalensis episcopi etymologiarum sive originum libri XX,* ed. W.M. Lindsay (1911; repr. Oxford 1957)
Ker	N.R. Ker, *Catalogue of Manuscripts Containing Anglo-Saxon* (Oxford 1957)
MGH	Monumenta Germaniae historica
NH	New Hymnal
OH	Old Hymnal
PL	Patrologia Latina
V	BL MS. Cotton Vespasian D XII
Wi	Winchester group

THE CANTERBURY HYMNAL

British Library MS. Additional 37517

folios 105r - 128r

I ORDINARIUM DE TEMPORE

Hymn 1

Use: Nocturns, Sundays during winter. 'Winter' is the time from
November 1 to Easter.
Literature: *AH* 51.24; Stev. 4; Wal. 262; Gneuss 269; Szov. 142, 214

105r   1   PRIMO DIERVM omnium,
            quo mundus extat conditus,
            uel quo resurgens conditor
            nos morte uicta liberet:

    5   Pulsis procul torporibus
            surgamus omnes ocius
            et nocte quęramus pium,
            sicut prophetam nouimus,

    9   Nostras preces ut audiat,
            suamque dextram porrigat,
            ut expiatos sordibus
            reddat polorum sedibus,

   13   Vt quique sacratissimo
            huius diei tempore
            horis quietis psallimus,
            donis beatis muneret.

1/ 4   *liberet: liberat* 'orig.'
      7   *pium:* sc. *deum*
      8   *sicut prophetam nouimus:* sc. *quaerere. propheta* is David; see
            Ps. 118:55.
    12   *polorum:* of the heavens
    13   *quique = quicumque*
    15   *psallimus:* we sing

17   Iam nunc, paterna claritas,
     té postulamus affatim, /
     absit libido sordidans
     omnisque actus noxius,

21   Ne feda sit uel lubrica
     compago nostri corporis,
     per quam auerni ignibus
     ipsi crememur acrius.

25   Ob hoc, redemptor, quesumus
     ut probra nostra deluas,
     uitę perennis commoda
     nobis benignus conferas,

29   Quo carnis actu exules,
     effecti ipsi cęlibes,
     ut prestolamur cernui,
     melos canamus glorię.

33   Presta, pater piissime,
     patrisque compar unicę
     cum spiritu paraclyto
     regnans per omne seculum.
     Amen.

23   *auerni:* of hell
29   *carnis actu exules:* 'exiled (i.e. removed) from the deeds of the
     flesh'
31   *ut prestolamur cernui:* sc. *finem nostrum. ut* seems to be used in
     a temporal sense here: 'While we are humbly waiting.' The Latin
     prose paraphrase in *V* has *sicut prestolamur cernui;* there is no
     comparison implied here, however.
33   *Presta:* sc. *hoc*
34   *unicę:* vocative 'only Son'
35   *paraclyto:* defender, advocate

Hymn 2

Use: Lauds, Sundays during winter. Throughout this ed. the term 'Lauds' translates the scribe's *matutina*. The term 'Matins' is confusing, since at various times during the Middle Ages it referred to Nocturns (prayers offered at 3 a.m. or 2 a.m.) and to Lauds (prayers offered at 6 a.m. or 4 a.m.).

Author: Ambrose

Literature: *AH* 50.11; Stev. 6; Wal. 30; Gneuss 271; Szov. 50 ff., 56 ff.

YMNUS AD MATUTINAM

1   Æterne rerum conditor,
noctem diemque qui regis,
et temporum das tempora,
ut alleues fastidium,

5   Preco diei iam sonat,
noctis profunde peruigil, //

105v   nocturna lux uiantibus,
a nocte noctem segregans.

9   Hoc excitatus lucifer
soluit polum caligine,
hoc omnis errorum chorus
uiam nocendi deserit;

2/ 5   *Preco diei* = *gallus*

6   *noctis profunde peruigil:* 'the watchman of the dark night.' The adjective is best taken as a noun here; see Lewis and Short's *Latin Dictionary* for *vigil* 'watchman, sentinel.'

5-8   The cock is described as the herald of the day, the watchman of the dark night, and, in a transferred sense, the light in the night (because he announces the coming of the light), who separates one part of the night from the other. Here and in the following stanzas the cock can hardly be distinguished from Christ, whom he symbolizes.

13 Hoc nauta uires colligit,
   pontique mitescunt freta,
   hoc ipsa petra æcclesiæ
   canente culpam deluit.

17 Surgamus ergo strenue:
   gallus iacentes excitat
   et somnolentos increpat,
   gallus negantes arguit.

21 Gallo canente spes redit,
   egris salus refunditur,
   mucro latronis conditur,
   lapsis fides reuertitur.

25 Iesu, pauentes respice
   et nos uidendo corrige;
   si respicis lapsus cadunt
   fletuque culpa soluitur.

29 Tú, lux, refulge sensibus
   mentisque somnum discute;
   te nostra uox primum sonet,/
   et uota soluamus tibi.

33 Deo patri sit gloria
   eiusque soli filio
   cum spiritu paraclyto
   et nunc et in perpetuum.
   Amen.

15 ff. After Peter (*petra æcclesiæ*) had denied Christ three times the
   cock crowed three times (*negantes arguit*, 20); Christ 'turned and
   looked upon Peter' (*nos uidendo corrige*, 26), and Peter 'wept
   bitterly' (*culpam deluit,* 16). See Lc. 22:55-62.

Hymn 3

Use: Nocturns, Sundays during summer
Author: Possibly Alcuin? See Wal. 265.
Literature: *AH* 51.26; Stev. 7; Wal. 265; Gneuss 273

(105v)   ITEM YMNUS AD NOCTURNAM

1   Nocte surgentes uigilemus omnes,
    semper in psalmis meditemur atque
    uiribus totis domino canamus
    dulciter hymnos,

5   Ut pio regi pariter canentes
    cum suis sanctis mereamur aulam
    ingredi cæli simul et beatam
    ducere uitam.

9   Prestet hoc nobis deitas beata
    patris et nati pariterque sancti
    spiritus, cuius reboat in omni
    gloria mundo.

Hymn 4

Use: Lauds, Sundays during summer
Author: Possibly Alcuin? See Wal. 265.
Literature: *AH* 51.31; Stev. 8; Wal. 276; Gneuss 273

          HYMNUS AD MATUTINAM

1   Ecce iam noctis tenuatur umbra,
    lucis aurora rutilans coruscat.//
106r nisibus totis rogitemus omnes
    cunctipotentem,

5   Vt deus nostri miseratus omnem
    pellat languorem, tribuat salutem,

4/ 4   *cunctipotentem:* Almighty

donet et patris pietate nobis
regna polorum.

9   Prestet hoc nobis.

Hymn 5

Use: Prime, daily
Literature: *AH* 51.40; Stev. 9; Wal. 293; Gneuss 274; Szov. 95, 116, 214

(106r)   HYMNUS AD PRIMAM

1   Iam lucis orto sidere
deum precemur supplices,
ut in diurnis actibus
nos seruet a nocentibus;

5   Linguam refrenans temperet
ne litis horror insonet,
uisum fouendo contegat
ne uanitates hauriat.

9   Sint pura cordis intima
absistat et uechordia,
carnis terat superbiam
potus cibique parcitas,

13   Vt, cum dies abscesserit
noctemque sors reduxerit,
mundi per abstinentiam
ipsi canamus gloriam.

17   Deo patri sit gloria. /

4/ 9   The doxology is that of Hymn 3.
5/ 15   *mundi per abstinentiam:*   through abstinence from the world
17   The doxology is that of Hymn 2.

Hymn 6

Use: Terce, daily except for Lent and Pentecost (see Hymns 47 and 65)
Author: Ambrose (?). See Szov. 51.
Literature: *AH* 50.19; Stev. 10; Wal. 109; Gneuss 275; Szov. 51, 214

(106r)   HYMNUS AD TERTIAM

1   Nunc sancte nobis spiritus,
     unus patris cum filio,
     dignare promtus ingeri
     nostro refusus pectori.

5   Ós, lingua, mens, sensus, uigor
     confessionem personet,
     flammescat igne caritas,
     accendat ardor proximos.

9   Presta, pater piissime.

Hymn 7

Use: Sext, daily except for Lent and Pentecost (see Hymns 48 and 65)
Author: Ambrose (?). See Szov. 51.
Literature: *AH* 50.20; Stev. 10; Wal. 110; Gneuss 275; Szov. 51, 214

(106r)   YMNUS AD SEXTAM

1   Rector potens, uerax deus,
     qui temperas rerum uices,
     splendore mane instruis
     et ignibus meridiem,

5   Extingue flammas litium,
     aufer calorem noxium,

6/ 9   The doxology is that of Hymn 1.

confer salutem corporum,
ueramque pacem cordium.

9   Presta, pater piissime.

Hymn 8

Use: None, daily except for Lent and Pentecost (see Hymns 49 and 65)
Author: Ambrose (?). See Szov. 51.
Literature: AH 50.20; Stev. 11; Wal. 111; Gneuss 276; Szov. 51

HYMNUS AD NONAM

1   Rerum deus, tenax uigor
inmotus in te permanet,
lucis diurne tempora
successibus determinans: //

106v 5   Largire clarum uespere,
quo uita nusquam decidat,
sed premium mortis sacrę
perhennis instet gloria.

9   Presta, pater piissime.

7/ 9   The doxology is that of Hymn 1.
8/ 2   *permanet: permanens* 'orig.' The slight difference in reading pro-
duces quite a difference in sense. B's text translates: 'O God of
the universe, the power which holds everything together remains
undiminished in you.' 'Orig.' introduces two different attributes
of God in the two lines: 'O God you are the strength that holds
together the universe, you remain immutable within yourself.'
6   *quo = ut*
9   The doxology is that of Hymn 1.

Hymn 9

Use: Vespers, Sundays
Literature: AH 51.34; Stev. 13; Wal. 280; Gneuss 279; Szov. 142, 214

(106v)   HYMNUS AD UESPERAM

1   Lucis creator optime,
         lucem dierum proferens,
         primordiis lucis nouę
         mundi parans originem,

5   Qui mane iunctum uesperi
         diem uocari precipis,
         tetrum chaos inlabitur:
         audi preces cum fletibus,

9   Ne mens grauata crimine
         uitę sit exul munere,
         dum nil perhenne cogitat
         seséque culpis illigat.

13   Cælorum pulset intimum,
         uitale tollat premium;
         uitemus omne noxium,
         purgemus omne pessimum.

17   Presta, pater piissime.

9/ 5-6   See Gen. 1:5.
     13   *pulset:* sc. *mens*
     17   The doxology is that of Hymn 1.

Hymn 10

Use: Compline, daily during summer (but see Hymn 11)
Literature: *AH* 51.42; Stev. 11; Wal. 299; Gneuss 277; Szov. 95, 214

(106v)   YMNUS AD COMPLETORIUM

1   Te lucis ante terminum,/
         rerum creator, poscimus,
         ut solita clementia
         sis presul ad custodiam.

5   Procul recedant somnia
         et noctium fantasmata,
         hostemque nostrum comprime
         ne polluantur corpora.

9   Presta, pater omnipotens,
         per Iesum Christum dominum,
         qui tecum in perpetuum
         regnat cum sancto spiritu.
         AMEN.

Hymn 11

Use: The rubric here is vague. Obviously Hymns 10 and 11 were not
         both chanted at Compline daily during summer. None of the
         other Ca or Wi MSS contains this hymn and thus can shed no
         light on its use. *AH* suggests that the hymn was used 'in aduentu';
         J. Mearns, *Early Latin Hymnaries: An Index of Hymns in Hym-
         naries before 1100* (Cambridge 1913; repr. Hildesheim 1970) p.
         47, suggests Advent and Easter. A use around Easter seems more
         likely, since Hymn 11 is paired with 10, another summer hymn.
Literature: *AH* 51.43; Stev. 165

10/ 6   *fantasmata:* apparitions, spectres

ITEM ALIUS YMNUS

1 Iesu, redemptor sæculi,
uerbum patris altissimi,
lux lucis inuisibilis,
custos tuorum peruigil,

5 Tu fabricator omnium
discretor atque temporum,
fessa labore corpora
noctis quiete recrea.

9 Te deprecamur supplices,
ut nos ab hoste liberes,
ne ualeat seducere
tuo redemptos sanguine,

13 Et, dum graui in corpore //
107r breui manemus tempore,
sic caro nostra dormiat,
ut mens sopore uigilet.

17 Deo patri sit gloria.

Hymn 12

Use: Compline, daily during winter (but see Hymn 13)
Literature: *AH* 51.21; Stev. 12; Wal. 259; Gneuss 278; Szov. 112, 118, 143, 214

11/ 3   See l. 4 of the Creed in the Appendix.
5   *fabricator:* creator
6   *discretor:* you who mark off
16   *sopore:* 'in sleep'; for the idea of wakefulness in sleep see Cant. 5:2.
17   The doxology is that of Hymn 2.

(107r)   YMNUS AD COMPLETORIUM

1   Christe, qui lux es et dies,
    noctis tenebras detegis,
    lucisque lumen crederis
    lumen beatum predicans,

5   Precamur, sancte domine,
    defende nos in hac nocte;
    sit nobis in te requies,
    quietam noctem tribue,

9   Ne grauis somnus inruat,
    ne hostis nos subripiat,
    ne caro illi consentiens
    nos tibi reos statuat.

13 Oculi somnum capiant,
    cor ad te semper uigilet,
    dextera tua protegat
    famulos qui te diligunt.

17 Defensor noster, aspice,
    insidiantes reprime,
    guberna tuos famulos
    quos sanguine mercatus és./

21 Memento nostri, domine,
    in graui isto corpore,
    qui es defensor animę
    adesto nobis, domine.

25 Deo patri sit gloria.

12/ 3   Cf. Hymn 11.3.
   11   *illi:* sc. *hosti*
   25   The doxology is that of Hymn 2.

Hymn 13

Use: The rubric for this hymn is vague. 12 and 13 are both winter hymns, but they are not interchangeable. Mearns (see Hymn 11) p. 25, suggests that this hymn was used at Compline during Lent.

Author: Prudentius. The hymn (minus doxology) constitutes the last seven stanzas of *Cathemerinon* VI.

Literature: AH 50.29; Wal. 130; Szov. 82 f., 93; CCSL 126.33

(107r) ITEM ALIUS

1 Cultor dei, memento
te fontis et lauacri
rorem subisse sanctum,
te crismate innouatum.

5 Fác, cum uocante somno
castum petis cubile,
frontem locumque cordis
crucis figura signet.

9 Crux pellit omne crimen,
fugiunt crucem tenebrę:
tali dicata somno
mens fluctuare nescit.

13 Procul, procul, uagantum
portenta somniorum!
procul esto peruicaci
prestigiator astu!

17 O tortuosę serpens,
qui mille per meandros
fraudesque flexuosas//
107v agitas quieta corda,

13/ 1 *Cultor:* worshipper
2-3 *fontis et lauacri rorem:* refers to baptism
4 *crismate innouatum:* refers to the sacrament of confirmation
16 *prestigiator:* deceiver
18 *meandros:* coils

21   Discede, Christus hic est,
hic Christus est, liquesce!
signum quod ipse nosti
damnat tuam cateruam.

25   Corpus licet fatiscens
iacet recline paulo,
Christum tamen sub ipso
meditamur sopore.

29   Deo patri sit gloria.

Hymn 14

Use: Nocturns, Mondays
Literature: *AH* 51.27; Stev. 14; Wal. 267; Gneuss 280; Szov. 142, 214

(107v)   HYMNUS AD NOCTURNAM

1   Somno refectis artubus
spreto cubili surgimus;
nobis, pater, canentibus
adesse té deposcimus.

5   Te lingua primum concinat,
te mentis ardor ambiat,
ut actuum sequentium
tu, sancte, sis exordium.

9   Cedant tenebræ lumini
et nox diurno sideri,
ut culpa quam nox intulit
lucis labascat munere.

13   Precamur idem supplices
noxas ut omnes amputes,/

13/ 29   The doxology is that of Hymn 2.
14/ 14   *noxas:* sins

et ore te canentium
lauderis in perpetuum.

17   Presta, pater piissime.

Hymn 15

Use: Lauds, Mondays
Author: Ambrose
Literature: *AH* 50.11; Stev. 15; Wal. 35; Gneuss 281; Szov. 51, 55 f.,
    58, 65 f., 143, 214

(107v)   HYMNUS AD MATUTINAM

1   Splendor paternę gloriæ,
      de luce lucem proferens,
      lux lucis et fons luminis,
      dies dierum inluminans,

5   Verusque sol illabere,
      micans nitore perpeti,
      iubarque sancti spiritus
      infunde nostris sensibus.

9   Uotis uocemus te patrem,
      patrem perhennis gloriæ,
      patrem potentis gratiæ, —
      culpam religet lubricam,

13   Informet actus strenuos,
      dentes retundat inuidi,
      casus secundet asperos,
      donet gerendi gratiam,

14/ 17   The doxology is that of Hymn 1.
15/ 2-3   Cf. Hymn 11.3.
    4   *dies dierum inluminans:* 'the light which illuminates all other
          lights.' The gen. regularly follows pres. part. of trans. verbs which
          are used adjectivally.
    5   *Verusque sol illabere:* sc. *in nos*
    12   *religet:* sc. *sanctus spiritus*

17   Mentem gubernet et regat
     casto fideli corpore;
     fides calore ferueat,
     fraudis uenena nesciat.

21   Christusque nobis sit cibus,//
108r potusque noster sit fides,
     leti bibamus sobrie
     ebrietatem spiritus.

25   Letus dies hic transeat,
     pudor sit ut diluculum,
     fides uelut meridies,
     crepusculum mens nesciat.

29   Aurora cursus prouehit,
     aurora tota prodeat,
     in patre totus filius
     et totus in uerbo pater.

33   Deo patri sit gloria.

Hymn 16

Use: Vespers, Mondays
Literature: *AH* 51.35; Stev. 17; Wal. 281; Gneuss 283; Szov. 142, 214

(108r)   FERIA .II. YMNUS AD UESPERAM

1   INMENSE cæli conditor,
     qui, mixta ne confunderent,
     aquę fluenta diuidens
     cælum dedisti limitem,

15/ 18   *casto fideli corpore* = *casto et fideli corpore*
   23-4   A reference to Pentecost; see Act. 2:13-15.
   32   *in uerbo:* i.e. *in filio* (see Io. 1:1)
   33   The doxology is that of Hymn 2.
16/ rubric *Feria:* week-day
   1-8   These lines are based on Gen. 1: 6-8.

5   Firmans locum cælestibus
     simulque terræ riuulis,
     ut unda flammas temperet,
     terrę solum ne dissipet,

9   Infunde nunc, piissime,
     donum perennis gratiæ,
     fraudis nouę ne casibus
     nos error atterat uetus.

13   Lucem fides inueniat,/
     sic luminis iubar ferat,
     hæc uana cuncta terreat,
     hanc falsa nulla comprimant.

17   Presta, pater piissime.

Hymn 17

Use: Nocturns, Tuesdays
Literature: *AH* 51.28; Stev. 18; Wal. 268; Gneuss 284; Szov. 142, 214

(108r)   HYMNUS AD NOCTURNAM

1   Consors paterni luminis,
     lux ipse lucis et dies,
     noctem canendo rumpimus;
     assiste postulantibus.

5   Aufer tenebras mentium,
     fuga cateruas demonum,
     expelle somnolentiam
     ne pigritantes obruat.

9   Sic, Christe, nobis omnibus
     indulgeas credentibus,

16/ 15   *hæc:* sc. *fides*
      16   *hanc:* sc. *fidem*
      17   The doxology is that of Hymn 1.
17/ 1-2   Cf. Hymn 11.3.

ut prosit exorantibus
quod precinentes psallimus.

13   Presta, pater piissime.

Hymn 18

Use: Lauds, Tuesdays
Author: Prudentius. The hymn consists of stanzas 1-2, 21, and 25 of
Cathemerinon I.
Literature: *AH* 50.23; Stev. 18; Wal. 117; Gneuss 285; Szov. 82, 86ff.,
214; CCSL 126.3

AD MATUTINAM

1   Ales, diei nuntius,
lucem propinquam precinit,
nos excitator mentium
iam Christus ad uitam uocat.

5   'Auferte,' clamat, 'lectulos
ægros, soporos, desides;//
castique recti ac sobrii
uigilate; iam sum proximus.'

9   Iesum ciamus uocibus
flentes, precantes sobriȩ:
intenta supplicatio
dormire cor mundum uetat.

13   Tu, Christe, somnum dissice,
tu rumpe noctis uincula,
tu solue peccatum uetus,
nouumque lumen ingere.

17   Deo patri sit gloria.

108v (in margin beside stanza 5)

17/ 13   The doxology is that of Hymn 1.
18/ 17   The doxology is that of Hymn 2.

Hymn 19

Use: Vespers, Tuesdays
Literature: *AH* 51.36; Stev. 19; Wal. 283; Gneuss 286; Szov. 142, 214

(108v)   HYMNUS AD UESPERAM. FERIA .III.

1   Telluris ingens conditor,
mundi solum qui eruens
pulsis aquæ molestiis
terram dedisti immobilem,

5   Ut germen aptum proferens,
fuluis decora floribus,
fecunda fructu sisteret
pastumque gratum redderet,

9   Mentis peruste uulnera
munda uirore gratiæ,
ut facta fletu deluat
motusque prauos atterat,

13   Iussis tuis obtemperet,/
nullis malis adproximet,
bonis repleri gaudeat
et mortis actum nesciat.

17   Presta, pater piissime,
patrisque compar unice.

19/ 1-8   These lines are based on Gen. 1:9-13.
1-10   Translate: 'Mighty creator of the earth, who, after the irksome
waters had been pushed back, drawing forth dry land gave us the
immovable earth, ... cleanse the wounds ...'
7   *sisteret:* here the same as *esset*
9   *peruste:* burnt completely
11   *deluat:* sc. *mens*
17   The doxology is that of Hymn 1.

Hymn 20

Use: Nocturns, Wednesdays
Literature: *AH* 51.28; Stev. 20; Wal. 269; Gneuss 287; Szov. 142, 214

(108v)   HYMNUS AD NOCTURNAM

1   Rerum creator optime
rectorque noster, respice:
nos a quiete noxia
mersos sopore libera.

5   Te, sancte Christe, poscimus,
ignosce tu criminibus;
ad confitendum surgimus
morasque noctis rumpimus.

9   Mentes manusque tollimus,
propheta sicut noctibus
nobis gerendum precipit,
Paulusque gestis censuit.

13   Vides malum quod gessimus,
occulta nostra pandimus,
preces gementes fundimus:
dimitte quod peccauimus.

17   Presta, pater piissime,
patrisque compar unice
cum spiritu paraclyto.//

20/ 10-11 See Ps. 118:62.
   12   In Act. 16:25 Paul and Silas are praying *media ... nocte;* thus
         Paul by his deeds (*gestis*) held the opinion (*censuit*) that one
         should pray in the middle of the night.
   17   The doxology is that of Hymn 1.

Hymn 21

Use: Lauds, Wednesdays
Author: Prudentius. The hymn consists of ll. 1-8, 48-9, 52, 57, 59-60,
and 67-8 of *Cathemerinon* II.
Literature: *AH* 50.23; Stev. 21; Wal. 119; Gneuss 288; Szov. 82, 86,
87, 88f., 214; CCSL 126.7

109r   YMNUS AD MATUTINAM

1   Nox et tenebrę et nubila,
    confusa mundi et turbida,
    lux intrat, albescit polus,
    Christus uenit, discedite.

5   Caligo terrę scinditur
    percussa solis spiculo,
    rebusque iam color redit
    uultu nitentis sideris.

9   Te, Christe, solum nouimus,
    te mente pura et simplici
    flendo, canendo quesumus:
    intende nostris sensibus.

13   Sunt multa fucis illita
    quę luce purgentur tua:
    tu, lux eói sideris,
    uultu sereno inlumina.

17   Deo patri sit gloria.

21/ 13   *fucis:* 'with rouge'; transf. 'with pretence'
   17   The doxology is that of Hymn 2.

Hymn 22

Use: Vespers, Wednesdays
Literature: *AH* 51.36; Stev. 22; Wal. 284; Gneuss 289; Szov. 142

(109r)   HYMNUS AD UESPERAM. FERIA .IIII.ta

1   Cæli DEUS SANCTISSIME,
       qui lucidum centrum poli
       candore pingis igneo,
       augens decora lumina,

5   Quarto die qui flammeam
       solis rotam constituens,/
       lunę ministrans ordinem,
       uagos recursus siderum,

9   Vt noctibus vel lumini
       diremptiones terminum,
       primordiis et mensium
       signum darent notissimum:

13   Inlumina cor hominum,
       absterge sordes mentium,
       resolue culpę uinculum,
       euerte moles criminum.

17   Presta, pater piissime.

22/ 1-12   These lines are based on Gen. 1:14-19.
       5-8   Note that this relative clause contains no finite verb.
       9-12   Translate: 'so that the divisions (i.e. of sun and moon) should set
               a limit to night and day, and act as a well-known sign for the
               beginnings of the months.' *V* and *D* read *diremptionis,* as does
               'orig.', and *daret (dares* 'orig.').
       17   The doxology is that of Hymn 1.

Hymn 23

Use: Nocturns, Thursdays
Literature: AH 51.29; Stev. 23; Wal. 271; Gneuss 290; Szov. 142, 214

AD NOCTURNAM

1   Nox atra rerum contegit
      terrę colores omnium;
      nos confitentes poscimus
      te, iuste iudex cordium,

5   Ut auferas piacula,
      sordesque mentis abluas,
      donesque, Christe, gratiam,
      ut arceantur crimina.

9   Mens ecce torpet impia,
      quam culpa mordet noxia;
      obscura gestit tollere
      et te, redemptor, querere.

13   Repelle tu caliginem //
.109v   intrinsecus quam maxime,
      ut in beato gaudeat
      se collocari lumine.

17   Presta, pater piissime.

23/ 11   *gestit:* sc. *mens*
    14   *intrinsecus:* within
    15   *gaudeat:* sc. *mens*
    17   The doxology is that of Hymn 1.

Hymn 24

Use: Lauds, Thursdays
Author: Prudentius. The hymn consists of ll. 25, 93-4, and 96-108 of
Cathemerinon II.
Literature: *AH* 50.24; Stev. 24; Wal. 121; Gneuss 291; Szov. 82, 87, 89,
214; CCSL 126.7

(109v)   YMNUS AD MATUTINAM

1   Lux ecce surgit aurea,
pallens fatiscit cecitas
quę nosmet in preceps diu
errore traxit deuio.

5   Hæc lux serenum conferat
purosque nos prestet sibi:
nihil loquamur subdolum,
uoluamus obscurum nihil.

9   Sic tota decurrat dies,
ne lingua mendax, nec manus
oculiue peccent lubrici,
ne noxa corpus inquinet.

13   Speculator adstat desuper,
qui nos diebus omnibus
actusque nostros prospicit
a luce prima in uesperum.

17   Deo patri sit gloria.

24/ 17   The doxology is that of Hymn 2.

Hymn 25

Use: Vespers, Thursdays
Literature: *AH* 51.37; Stev. 25; Wal. 286; Gneuss 292; Szov. 142, 214

(109v)   HYMNUS AD UESPERAM. FERIA .V.

1   Magne deus potentiæ,
        qui ex aquis ortum genus /
        partim remittis gurgiti,
        partim leuas in aera.

5   Dimersa lymphis inprimens,
        subuecta cælis irrogas,
        ut stirpe una prodita
        diuersa rapiant loca:

9   Largire cunctis seruulis,
        quos mundat unda sanguinis,
        nescire lapsum criminum
        nec ferre mortis tedium,

13   Vt culpa nullum deprimat,
        nullum leuet iactantia,
        elisa mens ne concidat,
        elata mens ne corruat.

17   Presta, pater piissime.

25/ 1-8   These lines are based on Gen. 1: 20-23.
     1   *Magne   = magnae*
     1-6   Translate: 'God of great power, you [who] send part of the
           creatures which were born in the water back into the deep, and
           you lift part of them into the air, pressing the submerged crea-
           tures into the water, you destine those borne aloft for the heav-
           ens, so that ...'
     6   *irrogas: inrogans* 'orig.'
     17   The doxology is that of Hymn 1.

Hymn 26

Use: Nocturns, Fridays
Literature: *AH* 51.29; Stev. 26; Wal. 272; Gneuss 293; Szov. 142, 214

AD NOCTURNAM

1   Tu trinitatis unitas,
orbem potenter qui regis,
attende laudum cantica,
quæ excubantes psallimus.

5   Nam lectulo consurgimus
noctis quieto tempore,
ut flagitemus uulnerum
a té medelam omnium,

9   Quo fraude quicquid demonum //
110r   in noctibus deliquimus,
abstergat illud cælitus
tuæ potestas gloriæ.

13   Nec corpus adsit sordidum,
nec torpor instet cordium
et criminis contagio
tepescat ardor spiritus.

17   Ob hoc, redemptor, quesumus,
reple tuo nos lumine,
per quod dierum circulis
nullis ruamur actibus.

21   Presta, pater piissime.

26/ 9   *Quo = ut*
21   The doxology is that of Hymn 1.

Hymn 27

Use: Lauds, Fridays
Literature: *AH* 51.32; Stev. 27; Wal. 277; Gneuss 294; Szov. 142, 214

(110r)   AD MATUTINAM

1   Æterna cæli gloria,
     beata spes mortalium,
     celsitonantis unice,
     castæque proles uirginis:

5   Dá dexteram surgentibus,
     exurgat et mens sobria
     flagransque in laude dei
     grates rependat debitas.

9   Ortus refulget lucifer
     sparsamque lucem nuntiat,
     cadit caligo noctium:
     lux sancta nos inluminet,/

13   Manensque nostris sensibus
     noctem repellat sæculi,
     omnique fine diei
     purgata seruet pectora.

17   Quesita iam primum fides
     radicet altis sensibus,
     secunda spes congaudeat:
     tunc maior extat Karitas.

21   Deo patri sit gloria.

27/ 3   *celsitonantis:* of the one who thunders on high (= 'of God')
   9-11   Wal. 277 f. changes *ortus* (l. 9) to *hortus*, *sparsamque* (10) to
          ipsamque, and *cadit* (11) to *kadit* in order to restore the alpha-
          betical sequence of this abecedarius.
   21   The doxology is that of Hymn 2.

Hymn 28

Use: Vespers, Fridays
Literature: *AH* 51. 38; Stev. 28; Wal. 287; Gneuss 295; Szov. 142, 214

FERIA .VI. HYMNUS AD UESPERAM

1   Plasmator hominis deus,
      qui cuncta solus ordinans
      humum iubes producere
      reptantis et fere genus,

5   Qui magna rerum corpora,
      dictu iubentis uiuida,
      ut seruiant per ordinem
      subdens dedisti homini:

9   Repelle a seruis tuis
      quicquid per inmunditiam
      aut moribus se suggerit
      aut actibus se interserit.

13   Dá gaudiorum premia,
      dá gratiarum munera,
      dissolue litis uincula,//
110v astringe pacis foedera.

17   Presta, pater piissime.

28/ 1-8   These lines are based on Gen. 1: 24-31.
      1   *Plasmator:*   creator
      4   *fere = ferae*
      5   *Qui:* sc. *dedisti* of l. 8
      6   *dictu:*   at the bidding
     17   The doxology is that of Hymn 1.

Hymn 29

Use: Nocturns, Saturdays
Literature: *AH* 51.30; Stev. 29; Wal. 274; Gneuss 296; Szov. 142, 214

(110v)   AD NOCTURNAM

1   Summę deus clementiæ
        mundique factor machinę,
        unus potentialiter
        trinusque personaliter,

5   Nostros, pius, cum canticis
        fletus benigne suscipe,
        quo corde puro sordibus
        té perfruamur largius.

9   Lumbos iecurque morbidum
        adure igni congruo,
        accincti ut sint perpetim
        luxu remoto pessimo,

13   Vt, quique horas noctium
        nunc concinendo rumpimus,
        donis beatę patriæ
        ditemur omnes affatim.

17   Presta, pater piissime.

Hymn 30

Use: Lauds, Saturdays
Literature: *AH* 51.34; Stev. 30; Wal. 279; Gneuss 297; Szov. 142, 214

29/ 3-4   *unus ... personaliter:* one in power but three in persons
     9-11   For *lumbos accingere* see Is. 32:11, Jer. 1:17, or Lc. 12:35.
     13   *quique = quicumque*
     17   The doxology is that of Hymn 1.

(110v)   YMNUS AD MATUTINAM

1   Aurora iam spargit polum,
         terris dies inlabitur,
         lucis resultat spiculum:
         discedat omne lubricum./

5   Fantasma noctis decidat,
         mentis reatus subruat,
         quicquid tenebris horridum
         nox attulit culpę cadat,

9   Vt mane illud ultimum,
         quod prestolamur cernui,
         in lucem nobis effluat,
         dum hoc canore concrepat.

13   Deo patri sit gloria.

Hymn 31

Use: Vespers, Holy Saturday, according to the rubric. Vespers, Satur-
        days during summer, according to the hymn's position in the
        Ordinarium de tempore and the fact that there are two hymns for
        Vespers on Saturdays (see Gneuss 60).
Author: Ambrose
Literature: *AH* 50.13; Stev. 2; Wal. 46; Gneuss 267; Szov. 50 ff., 56,
        65 f., 143, 213, 214, 239

(110v)   HYMNUS AD UESPERAM
              IN SABBATO SANCTO

1   DEUS creator omnium,
         polique rector, uestiens

30/ 12   *concrepat:* 'resounds with'; the subject is *mane illud ultimum*
        13   The doxology is that of Hymn 2.

diem decoro lumine,
noctem soporis gratia,

5   Artus solutos ut quíes
reddat laboris usui,
mentesque fessas alleuet
luctusque soluat anxios,

9   Grates peracto iam die
et noctis exortu preces,
uotis reos ut adiuues,
hymnum canentes soluimus.

13   Té cordis ima concinant,
té uox canora concrepet,//
te diligat castus amor,
te mens adoret sobria.

111r

17   Et cum profundo clauserit
diem caligo noctium,
fides tenebras nesciat
et nox fidei luceat.

21   Dormire mentem ne sinas,
dormire culpa nouerit,
castos fides refrigerans
somni uaporem temperet.

25   Exuta sensu lubrico
te cordis alta sompnient,

31/ 4   *noctem:* sc. *uestiens*

11   *uotis: uoti* 'orig.' Wal. translates: 'that Thou wouldest help us
who are bound by our vow.' Since *reus* in the Christian context
usually means 'sinner' (see Hymns 33.8, 57.9, etc.) and *uotum*
often means 'prayer' (e.g. 15.9), the passage in *B* is best trans-
lated: 'so that you help us sinners because of our prayers.'

17   *profundo:* 'in its depth'; *profunda* 'orig.'

26   *te ... sompnient:* let them dream of you

ne hostis inuidi dolo
pauor quietos suscitet.

29   Christum rogemus et patrem,
Christi patrisque spiritum,
unum potens per omnia,
foue precantes, trinitas.

Hymn 32

Use: Vespers, Saturdays during winter
Literature: *AH* 51.38; Stev. 1; Wal. 290; Gneuss 266; Szov. 142, 214

(111r)   ITEM ALIUS YMNUS

1   O lux, beata trinitas,
et principalis unitas,
iam sol recedit igneus:
infunde lumen cordibus.

5   Iam noctis tempus aduenit
noctem quietam tribuens: /
diluculo nos respice,
saluator unigenite.

9   Te mane laudent carmina,
te deprecemur uesperi,
te nostra supplex gloria
per cuncta laudet secula.

13   Deo patri sit gloria.

32/ 13   The doxology is that of Hymn 2.

Hymn 33

Use: Vespers, Advent
Literature: AH 51.46; Stev. 34; Wal. 300; Gneuss 298

(111r)   HYMNUS AD UESPERAM
                DE ADUENTU DOMINI

1   Conditor alme siderum,
        ęterna lux credentium,
        Christe, redemptor omnium,
        exaudi preces supplicum,

5   Qui, condolens interitu
        mortis perire seculum,
        saluasti mundum languidum,
        donans reis remedium,

9   Uergente mundi uespera,
        sicut sponsus de thalamo,
        egressus honestissima
        uirginis matris clausula.

13   Cuius forti potentiæ
        genu curuatur omnium:
        cęlestia, terrestria
        fatentur nutu subdita,//

111v 17   Occasum sol custodiens,
            luna pallorem retinens,
            candor in astris relucens
            certos obseruans limites.

33/ 6   *seculum:* the world
     10   See Ps. 18:6.
     14   *genu curuatur omnium: genu curuantur omnia* 'orig.'
     16   *fatentur:* sc. *se esse. nutu subdita:* subject to the divine will
     17-19 *sol, luna,* and *candor* stand in apposition to *cęlestia* (l. 15).

21   Te deprecamur, agie,
uenturi iudex seculi,
conserua nos in tempore
hostis a telis perfidi.

25   Laus, honor, uirtus, gloria
deo patri et filio
simul cum sancto spiritu
in sempiterna secula.
AMEN.

Hymn 34

Use: Nocturns, Advent
Literature: *AH* 51.48; Stev. 36; Wal. 302; Gneuss 300

(111v)   AD NOCTURNAM

1   Uerbum supernum prodiens,
a patre olim exiens,
qui natus orbi subuenis
cursu decliui temporis,

5   Inlumina nunc pectora
tuoque amore concrema,
audito ut preconio
sint pulsa tandem lubrica.

9   Iudexque cum post aderis
rimari facta pectoris,
reddens uicem pro abditis
iustisque regnum pro bonis,/

33/ 21   *agie:* holy
     22   See ll. 11 and 12 of the Creed in the Appendix.
34/ 1   *Uerbum:* Christ. See Io. 1:1.
      7   *V* has *audita ut preconia* in accordance with the rhyme scheme.
The construction in *V* is a nom. or acc. absolute.

13   Non demum artemur malis
      pro qualitate criminis,
      sed cum beatis compotes
      simus perhennes celibes.

17   Laus, honor, uirtus, gloria.

Hymn 35

Use: Lauds, Advent
Literature: *AH* 51.48; Stev. 37; Wal. 304; Gneuss 301

(111v)   HYMNUS AD MATUTINAM

1   Uox clara ecce intonat,
      obscura queque increpat,
      pellantur eminus somnia,
      ab ethrę Christus promicat.

5   Mens iam resurgat torpida,
      quę sorde extat saucia;
      sidus refulget iam nouum,
      ut tollat omne noxium.

9   E sursum agnus mittitur
      laxare gratis debitum;
      omnes pro indulgentia
      uocem demus cum lacrimis,

13   Secundo ut cum fulserit
      mundumque horror cinxerit,
      non pro reatu puniat
      sed pius nos tunc protegat.

17   <L>aus, honor, uirtus, gloria.

34, 35/ 17   The doxology is that of Hymn 33.
   35/ 3   *eminus* is to be regarded as a dissyllable for the sake of the metre.
        8-9   See Io. 1: 29.
        13   *Secundo:* 'for the second time,' i.e. at the second coming

Hymn 36

Use: Feastday of St. Andrew (November 30)
Author: Rabanus Maurus? See Szov. 222 and 226.
Literature: *AH* 50.201; Stev. 38; Gneuss 302; Szov. 222, 226

IN NATALE SANCTI ANDREĘ APOSTOLI

112r 1 Nobis ecce dies// ordine congruo
uenit nunc celebris, clarus, amabilis,
quo uictor super alta
ascendit prope sidera.

5 Andreas, domini sanctus apostolus
germanusque Petri, principis inclyti,
princeps ipse uirilis
consors martyrio fuit.

9 Piscator fuerat Petrus et Andreas;
post ambo rapiunt orbis et agmina,
uastant æquora mundi
ad regna atque trahunt poli.

13 Dum Christum comites gressibus et pares
exequant, pariter dogmata colligunt,
eius mortem secuntur
et uestigia per crucem.
AMEN.

36/ 9-12 Both Peter and Andrew were fishermen; when Jesus made them
his disciples he said: 'Follow me, and I will make you fishers of
men' (Mt. 4:19). See also Mc. 1:17 for the same account.

15 The third line in these stanzas is usually scanned – – – ᴗᴗ – ᴗ;
l. 15 does not correspond to this pattern. Since both *V* and *D* give
the same reading as *B* I have not changed the word *mortem* to one
which would scan (e.g. *fata*).

Hymn 37

Use: Vespers, Christmas
Literature: *AH* 51.49; Stev. 39; Wal. 306; Gneuss 304

(112r) HYMNUS IN NATALE DOMINI
AD UESPERAM

1 CHRISTE, REDEMPtor OMNIUM,
ex patre, patris unice,
solus ante principium
natus ineffabiliter,/

5 Tu lumen, tu splendor patris,
tu spes perhennis omnium,
intende quas fundunt preces
tui per orbem famuli.

9 Memento, salutis auctor,
quod nostri quondam corporis
ex inlibata uirgine
nascendo formam sumpseris.

13 Sic presens testatur dies
currens per anni circulum
quod solus a sede patris
mundi salus adueneris.

17 Hunc cęlum, terra, hunc mare,
hunc omne quod in eis est,
auctorem aduentus tui
laudat exultans cantico.

21 Nos quoque, qui sancto tuo
redempti sumus sanguine,
ob diem natalis tui
hymnum nouum concinimus.

37/ 17 *Hunc:* sc. *diem*

25 Gloria tibi, domine,
qui natus és de uirgine
cum patre et sancto spiritu
in sempiterna secula.
AMEN.

Hymn 38

Use: Nocturns, Christmas
Literature: *AH* 27.113; Stev. 40; Gneuss 306

HYMNUS AD NOCTURNAM //

112v 1 Surgentes ad te, domine,
atrę noctis silentio,
uigiliis obsequimur
patrum sequentes ordinem,

5 Quem nobis dereliquerunt
iure hereditario,
ministrantes excubiis
tibi, sancte paraclyte.

9 Pari cum patre clarus és,
cum Christo subtilissimus,
multis modis et spiritus
rex mysticus agnosceris.

13 Fragiles carne conspice,
quos ille antiquissimus
suis decepit artibus:
tuis trahe uirtutibus.

17 Grex tuus tibi deditus
non teneatur crimine,

38/ 14 *ille antiquissimus:* the devil

quem tuo, Christe, sanguine
uoluisti redimere.

21   Oues errantes preuide,
pastor bone piissime,
ad aulam celsitudinis
tuis reporta humeris.

25   Tabefactus et saucius/
abscedat princeps demonum,
perdat predam de faucibus
fur inportunis rabidus.

29   Exultet Christus dominus,
psallat chorus angelicus,
laudes sonans in organo
tér 'sanctus' dicat domino.

33   Gloria tibi dicimus,
pater; una cum filio,
simul cum sancto spiritu
in trina laude personet.
AMEN.

Hymn 39

Use: Lauds, Christmas
Literature: *AH* 14.26; Stev. 41; Gneuss 309

(112v)   AD MATUTINAM

1   Audi, redemptor gentium,
natalis tui gloriam,

38/ 21-2 See Io. 10:11.
      23-4 See Lc. 15:5.
      33   Cf. 45.14 and 46.7-8, which both have similar syntax. 'We
          address you with acclamations of praise.'
      36   The subject of *personet* is *pater:* 'May he (the Father) together
          with the Son and the Holy Ghost resound in threefold praise.'

Bethleem egressus a deo,
Mariæ partus uirginis,

5 Christe, uirtutum domine,
non ex uirile semine,
diuinitatis unius
consorsque sancti spiritus,

9 És potens omnium salus:
in te credentes libera,
fortis ubique in proelio,
nos peccatores eripe.

13 Genitum deum ex deo //
113r miramur in hoc corpore,
hominem deo similem,
mysterium mirabile.

17 Nam ut nos sancti, credimus,
obstupescunt et angeli
casto nascentem corpore
pastorem ex tribu Iuda.

21 Lumen refundens perditis
Iesse originem ducis,
mundus contactu carneo,
esse quod uoluisti es.

25 Natalis tui gaudium,
quod homo natus ex deo;
omnes fatemur filium,
regnum paternum permanens.

29 Perhennes laudes dicimus
patri deo cum filio,

39/ 3 *Bethleem:* locative
13 See l. 5 of the Creed in the Appendix.
22 See Mt. 1:5.
25 *Natalis tui gaudium:* sc. *est*
28 *regnum paternum permanens* is not in apposition to *filium.* Supply *et* between *filium* and *regnum.*

qui est uocatus Ægypto
per suos famulos deus.

33   Renati sancto spiritu
lumen uidemus muneris,
sic sequentes dominum
salui erimus iugiter.

37   Laus, honor, uirtus, gloria
deo patri et filio./

Hymn 40

Use: Vespers, feastday of St. Stephen (December 26)
Literature: *AH* 19.255; Stev. 47; Gneuss 316

(113r)   HYMNUS IN FESTIUITATE
SANCTI STEPHANI PROTOMARTYRIS

1   Iam rutilat sacrata dies et splendida ualde,
qua mundo colitur toto Stephanus protomartyr.

3   Namque dies hesterna deum conspexit in aruis
natum, hæc Stephanum celso peperit paradyso.

5   Sic Stephanus, dignus meritis et stemmatis illo,
quod nomen resonat, fulget decoratus honore.

7   Sanguineas miscens acies cum gente feroci,
hic uictor meruit claros retulisse triumphos.

9   Nos humiles, martyr redolens, te poscimus omnes
Horrendi facias hostis uacuisse malignas

39/ 31   See Mt. 2:15 and Os. 11:1.
     37   The doxology is that of Hymn 33.
40/   1   For the martyrdom of St. Stephen see Act. 6:8-15 and 7:1-59.
      4   *hæc:* sc. *dies*
      5   *stemmatis:* 'of the wreath'; the name Stephanus is derived from
           the Greek word *stephanos,* 'wreath, garland.'
      9   *redolens:* in the odour of sanctity

11   Insidias et, quam ueniam pro cede rependis,
113v   nostris hanc maculis// prono refer ore precamur

13   Sicque deo nato tribuas herere supernis,
      cui sit magnifice uirtus et honor sine fine.
      Amen.

Hymn 41

Use: Vespers, Epiphany (January 6)
Author: Sedulius. The hymn consists of the first seven stanzas of an
      abecedarius which progresses to the letter Z. See CSEL 10.163
      for the complete poem.
Literature: *AH* 50.58; Stev. 50; Wal. 151; Gneuss 320; Szov. 63,
      98 ff., 118

(113v)   HYMNUS AD UESPERAM
      IN EPIPHANIA DOMINI

1   A solis ortus cardine
     ad usque terræ limitem
     Christo canamus principi
     nato Maria uirgine.

5   Beatus auctor sæculi
     seruile corpus induit,
     ut caro carnem liberans
     ne perderet quod condidit.

9   Casta parentis uiscera
     cælestis intrat gratia;

40/ 10   *uacuisse:* to fall idle, to cease
    12   *maculis:* sins
    13   *tribuas:* sc. *nobis*
41/ 1ff.   Throughout this hymn Sedulius is alluding to Lc. 1: 26-2:17.
    7-8   *ut ... ne* = *ne; V* reads as in *B; D* reads *ut ... non.*
    9   *Casta,* the reading of *B, V,* and *D,* is unmetrical since the second
         a should be long. 'Orig.' has *Clausae puellae uiscera.*

uenter puellę baiolat
secreta quæ non nouerat.

13   Domus pudici pectoris
templum repente fit dei;
intacta nesciens uirum
uerbo concepit filium.

17   Enixa est puerpera,
quem Gabrihel predixerat,/
quem matris aluo gestiens
clausus Iohannes senserat.

21   Foeno iacere pertulit,
presepe non obhorruit,
paruoque lacte pastus est,
per quem nec ales esurit.

25   Gaudet chorus cęlestium
et angeli canunt deo,
palamque fit pastoribus
pastor, creator omnium.

29   Laus, honor, uirtus, gloria.

Hymn 42

Use: Lauds, Epiphany (January 6)
Author: Sedulius. Continuation of the abecedarius begun in Hymn 41.
Literature: See Hymn 41.

(113v)   YMNUS AD MATUTINAM

1   Hostis Herodes impie,
Christum uenire quid times?

41/ 29   The doxology is that of Hymn 33.
42/ 1-2   See Mt. 2:3.

non eripit mortalia,
qui regna dat cælestia.

5   Ibant magi qua uiderant
stellam sequentes preuiam;
lumen requirunt lumine,
deum fatentur munere.

9   Katerua matrum personat
conlisa deflens pignora,
quorum tyrannus milia
Christo sacrauit uictimam.

13   Lauacra puri gurgitis//
114r   cælestis agnus attigit;
peccata quæ non detulit
nos abluendo sustulit.

17   Miraculis dedit fidem
habere se deum patrem,
infirma sanans corpora
et suscitans cadauera.

21   Nouum genus potentiæ!
aquæ rubescunt ydriæ,
uinumque iussa fundere
mutauit unda originem.

25   Laus, honor, uirtus, gloria.

5   *qua = ubi. uiderant: uenerant* 'orig.'
5-6 See Mt. 2:9-11.
9-12 See Mt. 2:16.
10   *pignora:* children
12   *uictimam:* as an offering
13-16 See Mt. 3:13-17.
15   Translate: 'The sins which he did not bring down (on us), he took away by cleansing us.'
21-4 See Io. 2:1-11.
22   *ydriæ:* in the jug
25   The doxology is that of Hymn 33.

Hymn 43

Use: Vespers, Candlemas (February 2)
Author: Rabanus Maurus? See Szov. 222.
Literature: *AH* 50.206; Stev. 54; Gneuss 325; Szov. 222, 227

(114r)   IN PURIFICATIONE SANCTE MARIĘ

1   Quod chorus uatum uenerandus olim
       spiritu sancto cecinit repletus,
       in dei factum genitrice constat
       esse MARIA.

5   Hæc deum cæli dominumque terræ
       uirgo concepit peperitque uirgo
       atque post partum meruit manere
       inuiolata.

9   Quem senex iustus Simeon in ulnis
       in domo sumpsit domini gauisus,
       ob quod optatum / proprio uideret
       lumine Christum.

13   Tu libens uotis, <petimus,> precantum
       regis æterni genitrix faueto,
       clara que celsi renitens olimphi
       regna petisti.

17   Sit deo nostro decus et potestas,
       sit salus perpes, sit honor perhennis,
       qui poli summa residet in arce
       trinus et unus.

43/ 1   *uatum:* of the prophets
     4   *Maria* is in apposition to *in dei ... genitrice* (l. 3).
     9-12 See Lc. 2:25-35.
     15   *olimphi:* of heaven
     16   *petisti:* you have reached

Hymn 44

Use: Vespers, Septuagesima (third Sunday before Lent)
Literature: *AH* 51.52; Stev. 55; Gneuss 326; Szov. 218f., 221

IN SEPTUAGESIMA. AD UESPERAM

1   Alleluia dulce carmen,
      uox perhennis gaudii,
      alleluia laus suauis
      est choris cælestibus,
      quam canunt dei manentes
      in domo per sæcula.

7   Alleluia leta mater,
      conciuis Hierusalem,
      alleluia uox tuorum
      ciuium gaud<ent>ium;
      exules nos flere cogunt
      Babylonis flumina.

13   Alleluia non meremur
      nunc perhenne psallere,
      alleluia nos reatus//

114v   cogit intermittere;
      tempus instat quo peracta
      lugeamus crimina.

19   Unde laudando precamur
      te, beata trinitas,

44/ 1   This hymn constitutes a farewell to the 'Alleluia,' which is not
        chanted between Septuagesima and Easter except on special
        feastdays or saints' days.
   7-8   The Alleluia is personified as a 'leta mater' and as a fellow inhab-
        itant of the Heavenly Jerusalem. This latter personification is a
        reference to the fact that the Alleluia is chanted in heaven all the
        time, while there are periods when it is not sung on earth.
 11-12 See Ps. 136:1.

ut tuum nobis uidere
pascha des in etherę,
quo tibi leti canamus
alleluia perpetim.
AMEN.

Hymn 45

Use: Nocturns, Septuagesima (see Hymn 44)
Literature: *AH* 27.74; Stev. 57; Wal. 317 (Wal. prints Hymns 45 and 46
as one; 45 consists of Wal.'s stanzas 1-4 and 9); Gneuss 327

(114v)   YMNUS AD NOCTURNAM

1   Alleluia piis edite laudibus,
         ciues etherei, psallite nauiter,
         alleluia perhenne edite laudibus.

4   Hinc uos perpetui luminis accolas
         assumet resonans ymniferis choris;
         alleluia perhenne edite laudibus.

7   Vos urbs eximia suscipiet dei,
         quæ letis resonat cantibus excita;
         alleluia perhenne edite laudibus.

10   . Felici reditu gaudia sumite,
         reddentes domino glorificum melos,
         alleluia perhenne edite laudibus.

45/ 4-6   The participial phrase *resonans ymniferis choris,* 'the place re-
sounding with hymn-singing choirs,' seems to be the subject of
this stanza. The writer of *B* may have considered *resonans* as
modifying *urbs* of l. 7. 'Orig.' reads *accola* for *accolas.*

13   Te, Christe, celebret gloria uocibus
     nostris, omnipotens, hac tibi dicimus;
     alleluia perhenne edite laudibus./

Hymn 46

Use: Lauds, Septuagesima (see Hymn 44)
Literature: *AH* 27.75; Stev. 58; Wal. 318 (this hymn consists of stanzas
     5 and 7-9 of Wal. XCII); Gneuss 328

(114v)   YMNUS AD MATUTINAM

1   Almum sideree iam patrię decus
     uictores capitis, quo canor est iugis:
     alleluia perhenne edite laudibus.

4   Hoc fessis requies, hoc cibus et potus,
     oblectans, reducens haustibus affluis;
     alleluia perhenne edite laudibus.

7   Nos té suauisonis, conditor, affatim,
     rerum, carminibus laudeque pangimus;
     alleluia perhenne edite laudibus.

10   Te, Christe, celebret gloria.

45/ 14   *hac:* 'with it' = *gloria*
46/ 2   *capitis:* verb
             quo = ubi
     5   *reducens: reduces* 'orig.', to read: *oblectans reduces haustibus
             affluis*
     7-8   *rerum* belongs to *conditor*
     8   *pangimus:* we sing
     10   The doxology is that of Hymn 45.

Hymn 47

Use: Terce, daily during Lent
Literature: *AH* 51.64; Stev. 59; Wal. 330; Gneuss 329; Szov. 163, 214

HYMNUS AD .III. COTIDIE IN XL

1   Dei fide qua uiuimus,
spé perenni qua credimus,
per karitatis gratiam
Christo canamus gloriam,

5   Qui ductus hora tertia
ad passionis hostiam
crucis ferens suspendia
ouem reduxit perditam.

9   Precamur ergo subditi,
redemptione liberi,
ut eruat a sæculo //
115r   quos soluit a cyrographo.

13   Gloria tibi, trinitas,
æqualis una deitas
ante omnia secula
et nunc et in perpetuum.
Amen.

47/ rubric *XL = Quadragesima* = Lent. There are forty days in Lent because
Christ fasted forty days (see Mc. 1:13).
1-4   For the triad of *fides, spes,* and *caritas* see I Cor. 13.
5-7   See Mc. 15:25.
8   Lc. 15:4-6
12   *cyrographo:* 'a signed bond, an obligation under one's own hand.'
The idea is that the sinners have signed a pact with the devil and
that Christ frees them from their obligations. See Col. 2:14 and
also Wal. 257f. and Szov. 118.

Hymn 48

Use: Sext, daily during Lent
Literature: *AH* 51.65; Stev. 60; Wal. 331; Gneuss 330; Szov. 163, 214

(115r)   HYMNUS AD .VI. m

1   Meridie orandum est
         Christusque deprecandus est,
         ut iubeat nos edere
         de suo sancto corpore:

5   Vt ille sit laudabilis
         in uniuersis populis,
         ipse cælorum dominus,
         qui sedet in altissimis,

9   Detque nobis auxilium
         per angelos mirabiles,
         qui semper nos custodiant
         in omni uita sæculi.

13   Gloria tibi, trinitas.

Hymn 49

Use: None, daily during Lent
Literature: *AH* 51.16; Stev. 60; Wal. 244; Gneuss 331; Szov. 163, 214

(115r)   HYMNUS AD NONAM

1   Perfecto trino numero
         ternis horarum terminis,

48/ 8   See l. 10 of the Creed in the Appendix.
    13   The doxology is that of Hymn 47.
49/ 1-2 Literally: 'The threefold number having been completed in three
         periods of hours' = 'three times three hours having passed.'

> laudes canentes debitas
> nonam dicentes psallimus,

5   Sacrum dei mysterium/
puro tenentes pectore,
Petri magistri regulam
signo salutis proditam.

9   At nos psallamus spiritu
adherentes apostolis:
qui plantas habent debiles
Christi uirtute diligant.

13   Gloria tibi, trinitas.

Hymn 50

Use: Vespers, first and second Sundays in Lent (see Gneuss 240)
Literature: *AH* 11.18; Stev. 61; Wal. 335; Gneuss 332; Szov. 163, 214

(115r)   HYMNUS AD UESPERAM

1   Sic tér quaternis trahitur
horis dies ad uesperum,

49/ 7   *Petri ... regulam:* see Act. 3:12-26. Peter's entire sermon following
the healing of the lame man could be considered a 'regula,' but
maybe the author refers especially to verse 19: 'Poenitemini igi-
tur, et convertimini ut deleantur peccata vestra.'

9-12   The word *planta* suggests Act. 3:7. The sense here is: Let us praise
God, just as the lame man who had been cured by the apostles
went into the temple with them and praised God.

11-12   Translate: 'May they (the apostles) love those who have lame
legs' (lit. 'weak soles'). 'Orig.' reads *qui plantas adhuc debiles/
Christi virtute dirigant,* which Wal. translates: 'And may they
(the apostles) make straight our feet (ankles), that are yet weak,
by the power of Christ.'

13   The doxology is that of Hymn 47.

50/ 1   In some continental MSS the following stanza precedes our first
stanza: 'Ut nox tenebris obsita/ aequans per horas tempora/
ternis quater successibus/ reddit diem mortalibus.' This stanza is

occasu sol pronuntians
noctis redire tempora.

5 Nos ergo signo domini
tutemus claustra pectorum,
ne serpens ille callidus
intrandi temptet aditum,

9 Sed armis pudicitiæ
mens fulta uigil libere
sobrietate comite
hostem repellat improbum.

13 Sed nec ciborum crapula
tandem distentet corpora,
ne ui per somnum animam
ludificatam polluat.//

115v 17 Gloria tibi, trinitas.

Hymn 51

Use: Vespers, third and fourth Sundays in Lent (see Gneuss 240)
Literature: *AH* 51.53; Stev. 62; Wal. 320; Gneuss 333

(115v)   ITEM ALIUS YMNUS

1 Audi, benigne conditor,
nostras preces cum fletibus
in hoc sacro ieiunio
fusas quadragenario.

5 Scrutator alme cordium,
infirma tú scis uirium:

not found in English MSS.
50/ 3   *sol pronuntians* is in the nom. absolute.
5   *signo domini:* the sign of the cross
7   See Gen. 3:1.
17   The doxology is that of Hymn 47.

ad te reuersis exhibe
remissionis gratiam.

9   Multum quidem peccauimus,
sed parce confitentibus;
ad laudem tui nominis
confer medelam languidis.

13   Hic corpus extra conteri
dona per abstinentiam,
ieiunet ut mens sobria
a labe prorsus criminum.

17   Presta, beata trinitas,
concede, simplex unitas,
ut sint acceptabilia
ieiuniorum munera.

Hymn 52

Use: This hymn was used on two different occasions: part 1 (stanzas
1-4) at Nocturns on the first and second Sundays in Lent; part 2
(stanzas 5-8) at Lauds on the same days (see Gneuss 240).
Literature: *AH* 51.55; Stev. 63; Wal. 321

(115v)   ITEM ALIUS YMNUS

1   Ex more docti mystico
seruemus en ieiunium/
denum dierum circulo
ducto quater notissimo.

5   Lex et prophete primitus
hoc protulerunt, postmodum

52/ 5   *Lex:* see Ex. 34:28. *prophete:* see I Reg. 19:8.

Christus sacrauit, omnium
rex atque factor temporum.

9   Vtamur ergo parcius
uerbis, cibis, et potibus,
sompno, iocis, et artius
perstemus in custodia.

13   Uitemus autem pessima,
quę subruunt mentes uagas,
nullumque demus callido
hosti locum tyrannidis.

17   Dicamus omnes cernui,
clamemus atque singuli,
ploremus ante iudicem,
flectemus iram uindicem.

21   Nostris malis offendimus
tuam, deus, clementiam;
effunde nobis desuper,
remissor, indulgentiam.

25   Memento quod sumus tui
licet caduci plasmatis:
ne dés honorem nominis //
116r   tui, precamur, alteri.

29   Laxa malum quod fecimus,
auge bonum quod poscimus,
placere quo tandem tibi
possimus in perpetuum.

33   Presta, beata trinitas.

7   *Christus:* see Mc. 1:13.
20   *flectemus: flectamus* 'orig.'
25-6 *tui ... plasmatis:* of your creation
33   The doxology is that of Hymn 51.

Hymn 53

Use: Lauds, third and fourth Sundays in Lent (see Gneuss 240)
Literature: *AH* 51.58; Stev. 64; Wal. 325; Gneuss 336

(116r)   ITEM. ALIUS YMNUS

1   Iesu, quadragenariæ
         dicator abstinentiæ,
         qui ob salutem mentium
         hoc sanxeras ieiunium,

5   Quo paradyso redderes
         seruata parsimonia,
         quos inde gastrimargiæ
         huc inlecebra depulit.

9   Adesto nunc ecclesiæ,
         adesto penitentiæ,
         quæ pro suis excessibus
         orat profusis fletibus.

13   Tu retro acta crimina
         tua remitte gratia,
         et a futuris adhibe
         custodiam, mitissime,

17   Vt expiati annuis
         ieiuniorum uictimis/
         tendamus ad pascalia
         digne colenda gaudia.

21   Presta, pater, per filium,
         presta per almum spiritum
         cum his per ęuum triplici
         unus deus cognomine.
         Amen.

53/ 1-2   See Mc. 1:13.
     7   *gastrimargiæ:* of gluttony
     7-8   These lines allude to Gen. 3:1-6.
     13   *retro:* in the past

Hymn 54

Use: Nocturns, third and fourth Sundays in Lent (see Gneuss 240)
Literature: *AH* 51.57; Stev. 65; Wal. 324; Gneuss 337

(116r)   ITEM ALIUS YMNUS

1   Clarum decus ieiunii
         monstratur orbi cęlitus,
         quod Christus altor omnium
         cibis dicauit abstinens.

5   Hoc Moyses carus deo
         legisque lator factus est,
         hoc Heliam per aera
         curru leuauit igneo.

9   Hinc Danihel mysteria
         uictor leonum uiderat,
         per hoc amicus intimus
         sponsi Iohannes claruit.

13   Hæc nos sequi dona, deus,
         exempla parsimoniæ;
         tu robor auge mentium,
         dans spiritale gaudium.

17   Presta, pater, per filium,
         presta per almum spiritum.//

54/   3-4   See Mc. 1:13.
       5   *Hoc:* sc. *ieiunio*
       5-6   See Ex. 34:28.
       7   *hoc:* sc. *ieiunium;* see I Reg. 19:8.
       8   *curru ... igneo:* see II Reg. 2:11.
       9   *Hinc:* see Dan. 1:8.
       9-10   *mysteria ... uiderat:* see Dan. 2:19.
       10   *uictor leonum:* see Dan. 14:39.
       11-12 *amicus ... sponsi:* John the Baptist; see Io. 3:29.
       15   *robor = robur*
       17   The doxology is that of Hymn 53.

Hymn 55

Use: Vespers, feastday of St. Benedict (March 21)
Literature: *AH* 2.40 (which lacks ll. 25-32; but see also *AH* 14.63,
     which has nine additional stanzas between the sixth and seventh
     of this hymn); Stev. 69; Gneuss 342

116v   IN FESTIUITATE SANCTI BENE-
            DICTI ABBATIS

1   Christe, sanctorum decus atque uirtus,
       uita et forma, uia, lux et auctor,
       supplicum uota pariterque ymnum
       suscipe clemens,

5   Qui tuum dudum Benedictum ad te
       adtrahens mire segregasti mundo,
       ut probra mundi reprobare discens
       te sequeretur.

9   Cuius deuotum animum pueri
       gratia prestas fidei ualére,
       qua ualens mira precibus peregit
       mente fideli.

13   Dein extendens pedem in remotis
       ardua scandit, cruciare mallens/
       corporis artus iuuenilis ardens
       casto amore;

17   Imbuit posthinc homines beatos
       regulæ artis animos retundi,
       et iugo semper domini polorum
       subdere colla.

55/   rubric St. Benedict was the founder of the Benedictine order. For his
            life see Gregory the Great, *Dialogues,* trans. Odo J. Zimmerman,
            Fathers of the Church 39 (New York 1959) pp. 55-110.
      18   *artis:* with restrictions

21 E quibus Maurus, sedulus minister,
   gurgite ductum Placidum puerum
   obsequens patri latice leuatum
   æquore traxit.

25 Huius, ó Christe, meritis precamur
   arceas iram, tribuas fauorem,
   <gratiam prestes> ueniamque nobis,
   mitis ad omnes.

29 Prebe, oramus, deus alme rector,
   ut fides nostra// uitiis resistat
117r atque uirtutum studiis ministret
   pectore puro.

33 Gloriam patri resonemus omnes
   et tibi, Christe, genite superne,
   cum quibus sanctus simul et creator
   spiritus regnat.
   AMEN.

Hymn 56

Use: This hymn was separated into two parts: part 1 (stanzas 1-5) was
   sung at Vespers on the Feast of the Annunciation (March 25),
   part 2 (stanzas 6-8) at Lauds on the same day. The MS rubric reads
   Purificatione for *Adnuntiatione*, a scribal error.
Author: Possibly Venantius Fortunatus. See Wal. 194 and Szov. 139.
Literature: *AH* 50.86; Stev. 74; Wal. 198; Gneuss 347; Szov. 99, 129, 139f.

21-4 The boy Placidus, one of Benedict's monks, had fallen into a lake
   and was in danger of drowning. Benedict blessed Maurus, another
   monk, and sent him to rescue the boy. Maurus ran down to the
   lake and 'kept on running even over the water.' This miracle en-
   abled him to pull Placidus from the waves. See *Dialogues*, p. 69.
25 *Huius:* sc. *Benedicti*

(117r) HYMNUS AD UESPERAM. IN ADNUN-
TIATIONE SANCTĘ MARIAE

1 Quem terra, pontus, æthera
colunt, adorant, predicant,
trinam regentem machinam
claustrum Mariæ baiulat.

5 Cui luna, sol, et omnia
deseruiunt per tempora,
perfusa cæli gratia
gestant puellę uiscera.

9 <M>irantur ergo sæcula,
quod angelus fert semina,
quod aure uirgo concepit /
et corde credens parturit.

13 Beata mater munere,
cuius supernus artifex
mundum pugillo continens
uentris sub arca clausus est.

17 Benedicta cæli nuntio,
foecunda sancto spiritu,
desideratus gentibus
cuius per aluum fusus est,

21 O gloriosa femina
excelsa super sidera,
qui te creauit prouide
lactas sacrato ubere.

25 Quod Æva tristis abstulit
tu reddis almo germine;

56/ rubric This hymn is based on Lc. 1: 26-38.
1 *æthera:* nom. pl.
3 *trinam ... machinam:* object of *regentem;* the 'fabric of the world'
is threefold, consisting of earth, sea, and air.
23 *prouide:* adverb
24 *lactas:* you give suck

intrent ut astra flebiles
cæli fenestra facta és.

29   Tu regis alta ianua
et porta lucis fulgida:
uitam datam per uirginem,
gentes redempte, plaudite.

33   Gloria tibi, domine,
qui natus és.

Hymn 57

Use: Nocturns, Feast of the Annunciation (March 25)
Literature: *AH* 51.140; Stev. 76; Gneuss 349; Szov. 219f., 247

HYMNUS AD NOCTURNAM

1   Aue, maris stella,
dei mater alma //
117v   atque semper uirgo,
felix cæli porta.

5   Sumens illud 'aue'
Gabrihelis ore,
funda nos in pace
mutans Eue nomen.

9   Solue uincla reis,
profer lumen cecis,
mala nostra pelle,
bona cuncta posce.

13   Monstra te esse matrem,
sumat per te precem

56/ 29   *alta: alti* 'orig.'
33   The doxology is that of Hymn 37.
57/ 5-8   The author engages in wordplay, suggesting that by addressing Mary
with 'ave' Gabriel reversed the name 'Eva' and indicated that the
Virgin would reverse the calamity brought into the world by Eve.

　　　qui pro nobis natus
　　　tulit esse tuus.

17　Vitam presta puram,
　　　iter para tuum,
　　　ut uidentes Iesum
　　　semper conletemur.

21　Uirgo singularis,
　　　inter omnes mitis,
　　　nos culpis solutos
　　　mites fác et castos.

25　Sit laus deo patri,
　　　summo Christo decus,
　　　spiritui sancto /
　　　honor, tribus unus.
　　　Amen.

Hymn 58

Use:　This hymn was separated into two parts: part 1 (stanzas 1-4) was
　　　sung at Vespers during Holy Week up to Maundy Thursday, part
　　　2 (stanzas 5-8) at Nocturns during the same time.
Author:　Venantius Fortunatus
Literature:　*AH* 50.74; Stev. 78; Wal. 174; Gneuss 351; Szov. 129, 132,
　　　135 f., 203

(117v)　　　YMNUS AD UESPERAM

1　Uexilla regis prodeunt,
　　fulgent crucis mysteria,
　　quo carne carnis conditor
　　suspensus est patibulo.

5　Confixa clauis uiscera,
　　tendens manus, uestigia,

57/ 18　*V* and *D* read *tutum* for *tuum.*
58/ 4　*patibulo:* 'a fork-shaped yoke' = a cross
　　5　*uiscera:* here 'body'　　6　*uestigia:* here 'feet'

redemptionis gratia
hic immolata est hostia.

9   Quo uulneratus insuper
mucrone diro lanceæ;
ut nos lauaret crimine,
manauit unda sanguine.

13   Impleta sunt quę cecinit
Dauid fideli carmine
dicendo nationibus:
'regnauit a ligno deus.'

17   Arbor decora et fulgida,
ornata regis purpura,
electa digno stipite
tam sancta membra tangere.

21   Beata, cuius brachiis
pretium pependit sęcli!
Statera facta corporis//
118r   predamque tulit tartaro.

25   Fundens aroma cortice,
uincens saporem nectaris,
fæcunda fructu fertili
portas triumphum nobilem.

29   Salue, ara, salue, uictima,
de passionis gloria,
qua uita mortem pertulit,
pro morte uitam reddidit.

33   Deo patri sit gloria.

9   *Quo:* sc. *patibulo*
22   The metre here is problematical: *sęcli* ought to be *saeculi* for the
line to scan properly. This then requires *pretium* to be scanned
either as a dissyllable (*prĕtĭum*) or as a trisyllable (*prĕtĭŭm*), whereby the first two short syllables stand in place of one long one.
32   *pro: et* 'orig.'
33   The doxology is that of Hymn 2.

Hymn 59

Use: Lauds, Holy Week up to Maundy Thursday
Literature: *AH* 51.70; Stev. 79; Gneuss 353

(118r)   HYMNUS AD MATUTINAM

1   Auctor salutis unicus,
       mundi redemptor inclytus,
       tu, Christe, nobis annuam
       crucis secunda gloriam.

5   Tu sputa, colaphos, uincula,
       et dira passus uerbera,
       crucem uolens ascenderas
       nostræ salutis gratia.

9   Hinc morte mortem diruens
       uitamque uita largiens
       mortis ministrum subdolum
       deuiceras diabolum.

13   Nunc in parentis dextera
       sacrata fulgens uictima,/
       audi, precamur, uiuido
       tuo redemptos sanguine,

17   Quo te sequentes omnibus
       morum processu sęculis
       aduersus omne scandalum
       crucis feramus labarum.

21   Presta, beata trinitas.

59/ 4   *secunda:* imperative
    13   See l. i0 of the Creed in the Appendix.
    21   The doxology is that of Hymn 51.

Hymn 60

Use: Vespers, Easter
Literature: *AH* 51.87; Stev. 82; Wal. 350; Gneuss 354; Szov. 95, 163, 214

HYMNUS AD UESPERAM
IN PASCHA DOMINI

1   AD CENAM agni prouidi
       stolis albis candidi
       post transitum maris rubri
       Christo canamus principi.

5   Cuius sacrum corpusculum
       in ara crucis torridum
       cruore eius roseo
       gustando uiuimus deo,

9   Protecti pasche uespere
       a deuastante angelo,
       erepti de durissimo
       pharonis imperio.

13   Iam pascha nostrum Christus est,
       qui immolatus agnus est;//
118v   sinceritatis azima
       caro eius oblata est.

17   O uera digna hostia,
       per quam fracta sunt tartara,

60/ 1   *Ad cenam agni:* see Apoc. 19:9.
     7   *cruore:* sc. *cum*
     8   The object of *gustando* is *corpusculum.*
     9-12 See Ex. 12:1-51.
     15   *sinceritatis azima:* 'as the unleavened bread of sincerity'; see
          I Cor. 5:8.
     17-24 The Bible contains only a few allusions to Christ's harrowing of
          hell, e.g. Mt. 12:40, Eph. 4:8-10, Rom. 10:6-8, I Pt. 3:19. The
          sentence 'descendit ad inferos' nonetheless formed one article of

redempta plebs captiuata,
reddita uitæ premia.

21   Cum surgit Christus tumulo,
uictor redit de barathro,
tyrannum trudens uinculo
et reserans paradysum.

25   Quesumus, auctor omnium,
in hoc paschali gaudio
ab omni mortis impetu
tuum defendas populum.

29   Gloria tibi, domine,
qui surrexisti a mortuis,
cum patre et sancto spiritu
in sempiterna secula.
Amen.

Hymn 61

Use: Nocturns, Easter
Literature: *AH* 51.95; Stev. 83; Wal. 364; Gneuss 356; Szov. 18

(118v)   HYMNUS AD NOCTURNAM

1   Iesu, nostra redemptio,
amor et desiderium,
deus, creator omnium,
homo in fine temporum:

60/   the Apostles' Creed (this is a creed which was thought to have
been formulated by the apostles themselves; it differs only slightly from the Nicene Creed, which is given in the Appendix). See
also the *Gospel of Nicodemus,* ed. H.C. Kim, Toronto Medieval
Latin Texts 2 (Toronto 1973) p. 5.

22   *de barathro:* from hell

5   Quæ te uicit clementia,
    ut ferres nostra crimina/
    crudelem mortem patiens,
    ut nos a morte tolleres?

9   Inferni claustra penetrans,
    tuos captiuos redimens,
    uictor triumpho nobili
    ad dexteram patris resides.

13   Ipsa te cogat pietas,
    ut mala nostra superes
    parcendo, et uoti compotes
    nos tuo uultu saties.

17   Gloria tibi, domine,
    qui surrexisti.

Hymn 62

Use: Lauds, Easter
Literature: *AH* 51.89; Stev. 84; Wal. 356; Gneuss 357; Szov. 163, 214

(118v)   HYMNUS AD MATUTINAM

1   Aurora lucis rutilat,
    cælum laudibus intonat,
    mundus exultans iubilat,
    gemens infernus ululat,

5   Cum rex ille fortissimus
    mortis confractis uiribus

61/ 9-11   See note to Hymn 60.17-24.
      12   See l. 10 of the Creed in the Appendix.
      17   The doxology is that of Hymn 60.
62/ 4-8   See note to Hymn 60.17-24.

pede conculcans tartara
soluit catena miseros.

9   Ille, qui clausus lapide
custoditur sub milite,
triumphans pompa nobili
uictor surgit de funere.

13   Solutis iam gemitibus //
119r   et inferni doloribus,
quia surrexit dominus
resplendens clamat angelus.

17   Tristes erant apostoli
de néce summi domini,
quem poena mortis crudeli
serui dampnarunt impii.

21   Sermone blando angelus
predixit mulieribus:
'in Galilea dominus
uidendus est quantocius.'

25   Ille dum pergunt concite
apostolis hoc dicere,
uidentes eum uiuere
adorant pedes domini.

29   Quo agnito discipuli
in Galileam propere
pergunt uidere faciem
desideratam domini.

33   Claro paschali gaudio
sol mundo nitet radio,
cum Christum iam apostoli
uisu cernunt corporeo.

9-32   These lines are based on Mt. 27:62-28:17.

37   Ostensa sibi uulnera
      in Christi carne fulgida/
      resurrexisse dominum
      uoce fatentur publica.

41   Rex Christe clementissime,
      tu corda nostra posside,
      ut tibi laudes debitas
      reddamus omni tempore.

45   Gloria tibi, domine.

Hymn 63

Use: Vespers, Ascension Day (forty days after Easter)
Author: Bede. Only stanzas 1-2, 14-17, 30, and 31 of Bede's hymn are
      used for liturgical purposes. For the complete text, comprising 32
      stanzas, see *AH* 50.103. Stanza 7 of this hymn is not part of the
      text as composed by Bede.
Literature: *AH* 50.103; Stev. 87; Wal. 371; Gneuss 359

(119r)   HYMNUS AD UESPERAM. IN ASCEN-
          SIONE DOMINI

1   Hymnum canamus domino,
      ymni noui nunc personent:
      Christus nouo cum tramite
      ad patris ascendit thronum.

5   Transit triumpho nobili
      poli potenter culmina,

62/ 37-40   These lines are based on Lc. 24: 36-48.
     45   The doxology is that of Hymn 60.
63/ 1   This hymn is better known by the first line 'Hymnum canamus
             gloriae' which occurs in *V*.
     1-28   These lines are based on Act. 1: 9-11.

qui morte mortem absumpserat
derisus a mortalibus.

9   Apostoli tunc mystico
in monte stantes crismatis
cum matre clara uirgine
Iesu uidebant gloriam.

13   Ac prosecuti lumine
læto petentem sidera
lætis per auras cordibus
duxére regem sæculi.//

119v 17   Quos alloquentes angeli:
'quid astra stantes cernitis?
saluator hic est,' inquiunt,
'Iesus triumpho nobili.

21   A uobis ad cęlestia
qui regna nunc assumptus est,
uenturus inde sæculi
in fine iudex omnium.'

25   Sicque uenturum asserunt,
quemadmodum hunc uiderant
summa polorum culmina
scandere Iesum splendida.

29   Quo nos precamur tempore,
Iesu redemptor unice,
inter tuos in æthera
seruos benignus aggrega.

33   Da nobis illuc sedula
deuotione tendere,
quo te sedere cum patre
in arce regni credimus.

10   *monte ... crismatis:* Mount of Olives
13   *lumine:* 'with the eye'; here the sing. is used for the pl.

37   Gloria tibi, domine,
      qui ascendisti supra sidera.

Hymn 64

Use: Lauds, Ascension Day, according to *B. V* and *D* have a different
          hymn for Lauds, namely 'Aeterne rex altissime,' which is not in *B.*
          In *V* and *D* 'Optatus uotis omnium' is assigned to Nocturns.
Literature: *AH* 51.92; Stev. 89; Wal. 359; Gneuss 361

(119v)   AD MATUTINAM

1   Optatus uotis omnium
      sacratus inluxit dies
      quo mundi Christus spes, deus/
      conscendit cælos arduos.

5   Ascendens [in] altum dominus
      propriam ad sedem remeat;
      gauisa sunt cæli regna
      reditu unigeniti.

9   Magno triumpho prȩlii,
      mundi perempto principe,
      patris presentans uultibus
      uictricis carnis gloriam,

13   Est eleuatus in nubibus
      et spem fecit credentibus,
      aperiens paradysum
      quem protoplastis clauserat.

17   O grande cunctis gaudium,
      quod partus nostræ uirginis

63/ 37   The last two lines of the doxology are those of Hymn 60.
64/ 10   *mundi ... principe:* the devil
      16   *protoplastis:* dat. pl.; 'to the ones first formed' = to Adam and
            Eve. The 'orig.' reading *protoplasti clauserant* is an interesting
            alternative to the text here. In *B* it is Christ, while in 'orig.' it is

post sputa, flagra, post crucem
paternę sedi iungitur.

21 Agamus ergo gratias
nostræ salutis uindici,
nostrum quod corpus uexerit
sublimem ad cæli gloriam.

25 Sit nobis cum cælestibus
commune manens gaudium,
illis quod se presentauit,
nobis quod se non abstulit.//

120r 29 At nunc probatis actibus
Christum expectare nos decet,
uitaque tali uiuere,
quę cælos possit scandere.

33 Gloria tibi, domine.

Hymn 65

Use: This hymn was separated into three parts: part 1 (stanzas 1-3)
was assigned to Terce, part 2 (stanzas 4-6) to Sext, and part 3
(stanzas 7-9) to None. All three parts were sung at Pentecost
(fifty days after Easter).

Literature: *AH* 51.98; Stev. 95; Wal. 368; Gneuss 365

(120r) HYMNUS AD .III.
IN PENTECOSTEN

1 Iam Christus astra ascenderat,
regressus unde uenerat,

64/ Adam and Eve who close the gates of paradise after the Fall.
27-8 There is joy both in heaven and on earth because, even though
Christ presents himself in heaven, he does not absent himself
from earth.
33 The doxology is that of Hymn 63.

promisso patris munere
sanctum daturus spiritum.

5   Sollempnis urguebat dies,
quo mystico septemplici
orbis uolutus septies
signat beata tempora,

9   Cum hora cunctis tertia
repente mundus intonat,
orantibus apostolis
deum uenisse nuntiat.

13   De patris ergo lumine
decorus ignis almus est,
qui fida Christi pectora
calore uerbi compleuit.

17   Impleta gaudent uiscera
afflata sancto lumine,
uoces diuersę intonant/
fantes dei magnalia.

21   Ex omni gente coitur;
Grecis, Latinis, barbaris
cunctisque ammirantibus
linguis locuntur omnium.

25   Iudea tunc incredula,
uesano turba spiritu,

65/ 5-32   These lines, and Hymns 66-8 are based on Act. 2:1-41, the story
of Pentecost.

5   *urguebat: surgebat* 'orig.'

11   *orantibus apostolis:* 'orig.' *apostolis orantibus* is metrically better.

15   *Christi:* objective gen.; translate: 'believing in Christ.' *fida ...*
pectora: sc. *apostolorum*

16   *compleuit:* 'orig.' *compleat* is metrically better.

21-2   *coitur; Grecis, Latinis, barbaris:* 'orig.' reads *cogitur Graecus,*
Latinus, barbarus

24   *locuntur:* sc. *apostoli*

ructare musti crapulam
alumnos Christi concrepat.

29 Sed signis et uirtutibus
occurrit et docet Petrus
falsa profari perfidos,
Iohelis testimonio.

33 Hic, Christe, nunc paraclytus
per te pius nos uisitet,
terræ nouansque faciem
culpis solutos recreet.

Hymn 66

Use: Vespers, Pentecost
Literature: *AH* 50.193; Stev. 92; Wal. 374; Gneuss 363; Szov. 220f.,
222, 348

HYMNUS AD UESPERAM

1 Veni, creator spiritus,
mentes tuorum uisita,
imple superna gratia,
quę tu creasti pectora,

5 Qui paraclytus diceris,
donum dei altissimi,//
120v fons uiuus, ignis, karitas,
et spiritalis unctio.

9 Tu septiformis munere,
dexterę dei tu digitus,
tu rite promisso patris
sermone ditas guttura.

65/ 32 *Iohelis:* of the prophet Joel
33 *paraclytus:* here 'Holy Ghost'
37 The doxology 'Gloria tibi, domine' is erased.

13   Accende lumen sensibus,
      infunde amorem cordibus,
      infirma nostri corporis
      uirtute firmans perpeti.

17   Hostem repellas longius,
      pacemque dones protinus,
      ductore sic te preuio
      uitemus omne noxium.

21   Per te sciamus da patrem,
      noscamus atque filium,
      te utriusque spiritum
      credamus omni tempore.

25   Deo patri sit gloria
      eiusque soli filio.

Hymn 67

Use: Nocturns, Pentecost
Literature: *AH* 51.97; Stev. 93; Wal. 366; Gneuss 364; Szov. 348

(120v)   HYMNUS AD NOCTURNAM

1   Beata nobis gaudia
      anni reduxit orbita,
      cum spiritus paraclytus/
      effulsit in discipulos.

5   Ignis uibrante lumine
      linguæ figuram detulit,
      uerbis ut essent proflui
      et caritate feruidi.

9   Linguis locuntur omnium,
      turbæ pauent gentilium,

66/ 25   The doxology is that of Hymn 2.

musto madere deputant,
quos spiritus repleuerat.

13 Patrata sunt hæc mystica
pasche peracto tempore,
sacro dierum numero
quo legis fit remissio.

17 Te nunc, deus piissime,
uultu precamur cernuo,
inlapsa nobis cælitus
largire dona spiritus.

21 Dudum sacrata pectora
tua replesti gratia;
dimitte nunc peccamina
et da quieta tempora.

25 Sit laus patri cum genito
amborum et paraclyto;
proles ut hunc promiserat //
121r nobis modoque tribuat.
AMEN.

67/ 15 *sacro dierum numero:* sc. *quinquaginta;* Pentecost is the fiftieth
day after Easter.

16 *legis ... remissio:* 'orig.' *lege ... remissio* is metrically better. Both
versions translate: 'release from the law.' Every fifty years the Jews
had a jubilee year in which slaves were set free and debts forgiven.
The author of the hymn intimates that the fiftieth day after Easter
likewise is a jubilee day on which the faithful are cleared of their
debts, i.e. their sins, and freed from slavery under the devil.

27-8 Translate: 'as the Son had promised him (the Holy Ghost) so may
he give him to us now.'

Hymn 68

Use: Lauds, Pentecost
Literature: *AH* 23.35; Stev. 95

(121r)   AD MATUTINAM

1   Anni peractis mensibus
     tanta recurrunt gaudia,
     uotisque dudum credulis
     optatus aduenit dies,

5   In quo spiritus domini
     terras repleuit gaudiis,
     celestia aduentus sui
     mundo decurrunt lumina.

9   Sic namque filius dei
     apostolis spoponderat,
     celsos petisset cum polos,
     missurum sanctum spiritum.

13   Adest probatum testibus
     apostolorum uocibus,
     cum sint diuersis oribus
     uariis locuti gentibus.

17   Tanto redempti munere
     patris et nati spiritus
     iuges agamus gratias
     deo perenni in sæcula.
     AMEN.

68/ 9-12   See Act. 1:8.
     12   Construct: *se missurum esse sanctum spiritum.*
     13   *probatum:* possibly *probatus*, to modify *spiritus*. Both *V* and *D*
           read *probatum.*
     18   *patris et nati spiritus:* of the Spirit proceeding from the Father
           and the Son

Hymn 69

Use: This hymn was divided into three parts: part 1 (stanzas 1-4) was sung at Vespers, part 2 (stanzas 5-8) at Nocturns, and part 3 (stanzas 9-13) at Lauds on the feastday of St. John the Baptist (June 24). The scribe indicated this division by using slightly larger initial capitals at the beginnings of stanzas 5 and 9.

Author: Possibly Paulus Diaconus. See Szov. 186 ff.

Literature: *AH* 50.120; Stev. 102; Gneuss 368; Szov. 186 ff.

(121r)   YMNUS AD UESPERAM. IN NATALE
SANCTI IOHANNIS BAPTISTĘ /

1   Ut queant laxis resonare fibris
mira gestorum famuli tuorum,
solue polluti labii reatum,
SANCTE IohaNNES.

5   Nuntius celso ueniens Olimpho
te patri magno fore nasciturum,
nomen et uitæ seriem gerende
ordine promit.

9   Ille promissi dubius superni
perdidit promte modulos loquelę,
sed reformasti genitus peremptę
organa uocis.

13   Ventris obstruso positus cubili
senseras regem thalamo manentem;
hinc parens nati meritis uterque
abdita pandit.

17   Antra deserti teneris sub annis
ciuium turmas fugiens petisti,
ne leui saltem maculari uita
famine posset.

69/ 5-16 See Lc. 1:5-64.
17-24 See Mt. 3:1-6.

21   Prebuit yrtum tegimen camelus
      artubus sacris, stropheum bidentes,
      cui latex haustum, satiata pastum //
121v   mella locustis.

25   Ceteri tantum cecinere uatum
      corde presago iubar adfuturum,
      tu quidem mundi scelus auferentem
      indice prodis.

29   Non fuit uasti spatium per orbis
      sanctior quisquam genitus Iohanne,
      qui nefas sęcli meruit lauantem
      tingere limphis.

33   O nimis felix meritisque celse,
      nesciens labem niuei pudoris,
      prepotens martyr, heremique cultor,
      maxime uatum,

37   Serta ter denis alios coronant
      aucta crementis, duplicata quosdam,
      trino centeno cumulata fructu
      te, sacer, ornant.

41   Nunc potens nostri meritis opimis
      pectoris duros lapides repelle,

21   *yrtum:* rough, hairy
22-4   Supply *prebuerunt* with *bidentes* and *mella, prebuit* with *latex.*
23   *cui:* sc. *Iohanni*
25-8   See Io. 1: 29.
31-2   See Mt. 3:13-15.
35   *martyr:* see Mc. 6: 21-8 for an account of John the Baptist's death.
38   *duplicata quosdam:* i.e. sixty
37-40   The numbers here allude to those of Mt. 13: 23 or Lc. 8: 8. Chris-
      tian exegesis from St. Jerome onward identified 'thirtyfold fruit'
      with the married state, 'sixtyfold fruit' with the widowed state, and
      'hundredfold fruit' with virginity and, as for instance Theodulfus
      (MGH *Poetae* I, 471), martyrdom. See St. Jerome, *Adversus*
      Jovinianum I, PL 23.223-4; and Bede's commentary on Mt. 13,

asperum planes iter et reflexos
dirige gressus,

45   Vt pius mundi sator et redemptor
mentibus pulsa luuione puris
rite dignetur ueniens/ sacratos
ponere gressus.

49   Laudibus ciues celebrant superni
te, deus simplex pariterque trine,
supplices ac nos ueniam precamur,
parce redemptis.

53   Sit deo nostro decus et potestas,
sit salus perpes, sit honor perennis
qui poli summa residet in arce
trinus et unus.
AMEN.

Hymn 70

Use: Vespers, feastday of Sts. Peter and Paul (June 29)
Literature: *AH* 51.216; Stev. 105; Wal. 395; Gneuss 371; Szov. 122ff.,
174

(121v)   HYMNUS IN PASSIONE
PETRI ET PAULI

1   Aurea luce et decore roseo,
lux lucis, omne perfudisti seculum,
decorans cęlos inclyto martyrio
hac sacra die, quæ dat reis ueniam.

69/   PL 92.432. John the Baptist is here identified with the number
300, probably to show his pre-eminence among the saints.
46   *luuione:*   filth, foulness

5   Ianitor cæli, doctor orbis pariter,
     iudices sæcli, uera mundi lumina,
     per crucem alter, alter ense triumphat,
     uitæ senatum laureati possident.

9   Iam, bone pastor Petre, clemens accipe
     uota precantum, et peccati uincula
     resolue tibi potestate tradita,
122r   qua cunctis cælum // uerbo claudis, aperis.

13   Doctor egregie Paule, mores instrue
     et mente polum nos transferre satage,
     donec perfectum largiatur plenius,
     euacuato quod ex parte gerimus.

17   Oliue bine pietatis unice,
     fide deuotos, spe robustos, maximo
     fonte repletos caritatis gemine
     post mortem carnis impetrate uiuere.

21   Sit trinitati sempiterna gloria,
     honor, potestas, atque iubilatio,
     in unitate cui manet imperium
     extunc et modo per æterna secula.

70/ 5   *Ianitor cæli:* St. Peter (see Mt. 16:19). *doctor orbis:* St. Paul
    7   *per crucem:* St. Peter was crucified head down, on a cross that
        was turned upside down. For an account of his martyrdom see
        Edgar Hennecke, *New Testament Apocrypha,* ed. Wilhelm Schnee-
        melcher, trans. R. McL. Wilson (Philadelphia 1965) II, 318-22.
        ense: St. Paul was decapitated. See *New Testament Apocrypha,*
        pp. 383-7.
  9-12 These lines are also used for the first stanza of Hymn 81.
 10-12 See Mt. 16:19.
 13-16 These lines are also used for the first stanza of Hymn 82.
   16   Translate: 'that which we [now] do in part (i.e. imperfectly)
        having been abandoned.' See I Cor. 13:10.
   17   *Oliue:* see Apoc. 11:4.

Hymn 71

Use: Vespers, feastday of St. Laurence (August 10)
Literature: *AH* 50.193; Stev. 106

(122r)   HYMNUS DE SANCTO LAURENTIO

1   Martyris Christi colimus triumphum,
     annuum tempus uenerando cuius
     cernua uocis prece iam rotundus
     orbis adorat.

5   Pontifex Syxtus monuit ministrum
     fixus in ligno crucis: 'exequeris
     me cito, poenam patiendo magnam /
     ibis ad astra.'

9   Tortor iratus petit ut talenti
     pondus ignoti manifestet omne
     mente uesana cupiens uorare
     aurea lucra.

13   Spreuit hic mundi peritura dona,
     fert opem nudis, alimenta claudis,
     diuidit nummos miseris cateruis
     corde flagranti.

71/ rubric For the legend of St. Laurence see the Ambrosian hymn 'Aposto-
     lorum supparem' (Wal. 101) and Prudentius' *Peristephanon* II,
     and also the summary by Wal. 97-100. Briefly, the story is this:
     after Pope Sixtus II had been crucified during the persecution
     under Valerian (A.D. 258), Laurence, the archdeacon, was the
     chief personage in the Catholic church. The 'tortor,' i.e. the pre-
     fect who was to condemn Laurence to his death, demanded to
     receive all the treasures of the church. Laurence, however, distri-
     buted all the possessions of the church to the poor, and showed
     the poor to the prefect. Angered, the prefect ordered Laurence
     to be roasted on a gridiron.
10   *ignoti:* the 'tortor' did not know how much money the church had.

17   Igne torquetur, stabili tenore
cordis accensus superat minaces
ignium flammas in amore uitę
semper opime.

21   Uritur post hæc latus omne testis:
'uerte,' prefecto loquitur iocunde,
'corporis partem laniando coctam
dentibus atris.'

25   Spiritum sumpsit chorus angelorum,
intulit cęlo pie laureandum,
ut scelus laxet hominum precando
omnipotentem.

29   Supplici uoto rogitemus omnes,
sancte Laurenti, ueniam precéris,

122v   qui tuum festum celebrant // ubique
uoce uel actu.

33   Gloriam patri resonemus omnes
eius et nato iubilemus apte,
cum quibus regnat simul et creator
spiritus almus.

Hymn 72

Use: Vespers, feastday of St. Michael (September 29)
Literature: *AH* 14.83; Stev. 113; Gneuss 378

(122v)   YMNUS IN SOLLEMPNITATE
SANCTI MICHAELIS ARCHANGELI

1   Misteriorum signifer
celestium archangele,

71/ 21   *testis:* literally 'witness.' The Greek word for 'witness' is *martys.*
A person who suffers death for God is a witness for God, and
therefore 'testis' is a synonym for 'martyr.'

te supplicantes quesumus
ut nos placatus uisites.

5 Ipse cum sanctis angelis,
cum iustis, cum apostolis,
inlustra locum iugiter
quo nunc orantes degimus.

9 Castissimórum omnium,
doctorum ac pontificum,
pro nobis preces profluas
deuotus offer domino,

13 Hostem repellat ut sæuum
opemque pacis dirigat
et nostra simul pectora
fides perfecta perlustret.

17 Ascendant nostræ protinus /
ad thronum uoces gloriæ
mentesque nostras erigat,
qui sede splendet fulgida.

21 Hic uirtus eius maneat,
hic firma flagret caritas,
hic ad salutis commoda
suis occurrat famulis.

25 Errores omnes auferat
uagosque sensus corrigat
et dirigat uestigia
nostra pacis per semitam.

29 Lucis in arce fulgida
hæc sacra scribat carmina,
nostraque simul nomina
in libro uitę conserat.
Amen.

Hymn 73

Use: Nocturns, feastday of St. Michael (September 29)
Author: Rabanus Maurus? See Szov. 222.
Literature: *AH* 50.207; Stev. 114; Gneuss 380; Szov. 222, 227

AD NOCTURNAM

1   Tibi, Christe, splendor patris,
uita ac uirtus cordium,
in conspectu angelorum
uotis, uoce psallimus,
alternantes concrepando
melos damus uocibus.

7   Conlaudamus uenerantes
omnes cæli milites, //
123r   sed precipue primatem
cęlestis exercitus,
Michaelem in uirtute
conterentem zabulum.

13   Quo custode procul pellens,
rex Christe piissime,
omne nefas inimici,
mundos corde et corpore
paradyso redde tuo
nos sola clementia.

19   Gloriam patri melodis
personemus uocibus,
gloriam Christo canamus,
gloriam paraclyto,
qui deus trinus et unus
extat ante sæcula.
AMEN.

73/ 12   *zabulum = diabolum*

Hymn 74

Use: Lauds, feastday of St. Michael (September 29)
Author: Rabanus Maurus? See Szov. 222.
Literature: *AH* 50.197; Stev. 116; Gneuss 381; Szov. 222, 225

(123r)   AD MATUTINAM

1   Christe, sanctorum decus angelorum,
        auctor humani generisque rector,
        nobis æternum tribue benignus
        scandere regnum.

5   Angelum pacis Michael ad istam
        celitus mitti rogitemus aulam,
        nobis/ ut crebro ueniant et crescant
        prospera cuncta;

9   Angelus fortis Gabriel, ut hostem
        pellat antiquum, uolitet ab alto,
        sepius templum ueniat ad istud
        uisere nostrum.

13   Angelum nobis, medicum salutis,
        mitte de cęlis Raphael, ut omnes
        sanet egrotos pariterque nostros
        dirigat actus.

17   Hic dei nostri genetrix Maria
        totus et nobis chorus angelorum
        semper adsistat simul et beata
        contio tota.

21   Prestet hoc nobis deitas beata.

74/ 20   *contio tota:* sc. *omnium sanctorum*
    21   The doxology is that of Hymn 3.

Hymn 75

Use: Vespers, All Saints' Day (November 1)
Literature: *AH* 51.152; Stev. 117; Gneuss 382

YMNUS IN FESTIUI-
TATE OMNIUM SANCTORUM

1   Festiua sęclis colitur
    dies sanctorum omnium,
    qui regnant in celestibus,
    Iesu, tecum feliciter.

5   Hos inuocamus cernui
    teque, redemptor omnium;//
123v   illis tibique supplices
    preces gementes fundimus.

9   Iesu, saluator sæculi,
    redemtor ope subuenis,
    et, pia dei genitrix,
    salutem posce miseris.

13 Cætus omnes angelici,
    patriarcharum cunei,
    et prophetarum merita
    nobis precentur ueniam.

17 Baptista Christi preuius
    et clauiger æthereus
    cum ceteris apostolis
    nos soluant nexu criminis.

21 Chorus sacratus martyrum,
    confessio sacerdotum,

75/ 13   *Cætus = coetus*
    17   *Baptista Christi preuius:* St. John the Baptist, forerunner of Christ
    18   *clauiger æthereus:* St. Peter

et uirginalis castitas
nos a peccatis abluant.

25   Monachorum suffragia
omnesque ciues cælici
annuant uotis supplicum
et uitę poscant premium.

29   Laus, honor, uirtus, gloria
deo patri et filio.

Hymn 76

Use: Nocturns, All Saints' Day (November 1)
Literature: *AH* 51.150; Stev. 119; Gneuss 384; Szov. 342, 348

(123v)   HYMNUS AD N<OCTURNAM>/

1   Christe, redemptor omnium,
conserua tuos famulos,
beatę semper uirginis
placatus sanctis precibus.

5   Beata quoque agmina
cælestium spirituum,
preterita, presentia,
futura mala pellite.

9   Vates æterni iudicis
apostolique domini,
suppliciter exposcimus
saluari uestris precibus.

13   Martyres dei inclyti
confessoresque lucidi,
<uestris orationibus>
nos ferte in cęlestibus.

75/ 29   The doxology is that of Hymn 33.
76/ 9   *Vates:* prophets

17   Chorus sanctarum uirginum
      monachorumque omnium,
      simul cum sanctis omnibus
      consortes Christi facite.

21   Gentem auferte perfidam
      credentium de finibus,
      ut Christi laudes debitas
      persoluamus alacriter.

25   Gloria patri ingenito
      eiusque unigenito //
124r uná cum sancto spiritu
      in sempiterna sęcula.
      Amen.

Hymn 77

Use: Lauds, All Saints' Day (November 1)
Literature: *AH* 11.61; Stev. 120; Gneuss 385; Szov. 343

(124r)   HYMNUS AD MATUTINAM

1   Omnium, Christe, pariter tuorum
      festa sanctorum colimus precantes
      hos, tibi qui iam meruere iungi,
      nostra tueri.

5   Vincla nostrorum scelerum resoluant,
      luce uirtutum populos adornent,
      uendicent nobis pietate sola
      regna superna,

9   Et quibus uitæ stadium magistris
      curritur, horum precibus beatis

76/ 20   *facite:* sc. *nos*
77/ 9-10 Translate: 'and through the blessed prayers of those with whom
          as masters the race of life is run.'

fulgido cęli gremio locemur
perpete uita.

13   Gloriam sanctæ pię trinitati
turba resultet, canat et reuoluat,
quę manens regnat deus unus omni
tempore sęcli.
AMEN.

Hymn 78

Use: Vespers, feastday of St. Martin (November 11)
Literature: *AH* 27.218; Stev. 121; Szov. 321

(124r)   IN FESTIUITATE SANCTI MARTINI

1   Martine, confessor dei,
ualens uigore spiritus,
carnis fatiscens artubus,
mortis futuræ prescius, /

5   Qui in pace æcclesiæ,
in unitate spiritus
diuisa membra æcclesiæ
paci reformas unice,

9   Quem uita fert probabilem,
quem mors cruenta non ledet,
qui callidi uersutias
in mortis hora derogat,

13   Hæc plebs, fide promtissima,
tui diei gaudia
uotis colit fidelibus;
adesto mitis omnibus.

78/   rubric For a life of St. Martin see Sulpicius Severus, *Vita S. Martini,*
CSEL 1 (Vienna 1876) pp. 107-37.

17   Per te quies sit temporum,
      uitę detur solacium,
      pacis redundet commodum,
      sedetur omne scandalum,

21   Et karitatis gratia
      sic affluamus spiritu,
      quo corde cum suspiriis
      Christum sequamur intimis.

25   <D>eo patri sit gloria.

25   The doxology is that of Hymn 2.

III COMMUNE SANCTORUM

Hymn 79

Use: The use of Hymns 79, 80, and 81-90 is uncertain. Hymn 80 is
prescribed for Nocturns, and its content suggests that it be sung
on the feastday of any martyr, not on that of any apostle. If 80
was indeed used at Nocturns on the feastday of any apostle (as
it could have been, since all apostles except John were martyrs),
Hymn 79 may have been used at Lauds and Hymns 81-90 at
Vespers (to parallel the Wi use: see Gneuss 67).

Literature: *AH* 51.125; Stev. 122; Gneuss 386; Szov. 342

HYMNUS IN SOLLEMPNITATE
OMNIUM APOSTOLORUM

1 EXULTET cælum laudibus,//
124v resultet terra gaudiis,
 apostolorum gloriam
 sacra canunt sollemnia.

5 Vos, sæcli iusti iudices
 et uera mundi lumina,
 uotis precamur cordium,
 audite preces supplicum.

9 Qui cælum uerbo clauditis
 serasque eius soluitis,
 nos a peccatis omnibus
 soluite iussu, quesumus.

13 Quorum precepto subditur
 salus et languor hominum,
 sanate ægros moribus
 nos reddentes uirtutibus,

17 Vt, cum iudex aduenerit
 Christus in fine sęculi,

nos sempiterni gaudii
faciat esse compotes.

21   Deo patri sit gloria.

Hymn 80

Use: See Hymn 79.
Author: Ambrose
Literature: *AH* 50.19; Stev. 123; Wal. 105; Gneuss 392; Szov. 50 ff., 62, 65, 66, 116, 214

(124v)   HYMNUS AD NOCTURNAM

1   Æterna Christi munera
et martyrum uictorias,
laudes ferentes debitas
leti canamus mentibus./

5   Ækclesiarum principes
[et] belli triumphalis duces,
cęlestis aulæ milites
et uera mundi lumina,

9   Terrore, uita sæculi
penisque spretis corporis,
mortis sacræ compendio
uitam beatam possident.

13   Traduntur igni martyres
et bestiarum dentibus,

79/ 21   The doxology is that of Hymn 2.
80/ 6   The line is metrically better if *et* is omitted.
9-10   *spretis* modifies *terrore, uita,* and *penis.* Instead of *uita saeculi* ('the life in this world') 'orig.' reads *terrore uicto saeculi* ('the terror of this world having been defeated').
11   *compendio:* through the short cut

armata seuit ungulis
tortoris insani manus,

17 Nudata pendent uiscera,
sanguis sacratus funditur,
sed permanent immobiles
uitæ perhennis gratia.

21 Deuota sanctorum fides,
inuicta spes credentium,
perfecta Christi karitas
mundi triumphat principem.

25 In his paterna gloria,
in his uoluntas spiritus,
exultat in his filius,
cęlum repletur gaudiis.

29 Te nunc, redemptor, quesumus,//
125r   ut martyrum consortio
iungas precantes seruulos
in sempiterna sæcula.

Hymn 81

Use: Feastday of St. Peter (June 29). See Hymn 79.
Literature: *AH* 51.121; Stev. 124; Gneuss 371 for the first stanza, 387
for the remainder

(125r)   HYMNUS DE SANCTO PETRO APOSTOLO

1 Iam, bone pastor Petre, clemens accipe
uota precantum, et peccati uincula
resolue tibi potestate tradita,
qua cunctis cælum uerbo claudis, aperis.

80/ 24   *mundi triumphat principem:* triumphs over the devil
81/ 1-4 Cf. Hymn 70.9-12.

5   Annue, Christe, seculorum domine,
nobis per horum tibi kara merita,
ut quę te coram grauiter deliquimus
horum soluantur gloriosis precibus.

9   Salua, redemptor, plasma tuum nobile
signatum sancto uultus tui lumine,
nec lacerari sinas fraude demonum
propter quod mortis exsoluisti pretium.

13   Dole captiuos esse tuos seruulos,
absolue reos, compeditos erige
et quos cruore redemisti proprio,
rex bone,/ tecum fac gaudere perpetim.

17   Sit tibi, Iesu benedicte domine,
gloria, uirtus, honor, et imperium
uná cum patre sanctoque paraclyto
cum quibus regnat deus ante secula.

Hymn 82

Use: Feastday of St. Paul (June 30). See Hymn 79.
Literature: *AH* 51.121; Stev. 125; Gneuss 372

(125r)   HYMNUS DE SANCTO PAULO APOSTOLO

1   Doctor egregie Paule, mores instrue
et mente polo nos transferre satage,
donec perfectum largiatur plenius,
euacuato quod ex parte gerimus.

5   Annue, Christe.

81/ 6   *horum:* sc. *apostolorum*
9   *plasma:* creature
82/ 1-4   Cf. Hymn 70.13-16.
5   According to Gneuss 387 the text of Hymn 81.5-20, not just
5-8, follows here.

Hymn̈ 83

Use: Feastday of St. Andrew (November 30). See Hymns 79 and 36.
Literature: *AH* 51.121; Stev. 126; Gneuss 388

(125r) HYMNUS DE SANCTO ANDREA

1   ANdreas pie, sanctorum mitissime,
    optine nostris erratibus ueniam
    et, qui grauamur sarcina peccaminum,
    subleua tuis intercessionibus.

5   Annue.

Hymn 84

Use: Feastdays of Sts. James the Greater (July 25) and John (December 27). James and John were brothers and are therefore celebrated in one hymn. See Hymn 79.
Literature: *AH* 51.121; Stev. 126; Gneuss 388

    DE SANCTO IACOBO ET IOHANNE

1   Bina celestis aulæ luminaria,
    Iacobe necnon Iohannes theologe,
125v   poscite // nobis ueniam rogantibus,
    quam uenit Christus gratis dare miseris.

5   Annue.

83/ 2   *erratibus = erroribus*
    5   See Hymn 82.5 n.
84/ 5   See Hymn 82.5 n.

Hymn 85

Use: Feastday of St. James the Less (May 1). See Hymn 79.
Literature: *AH* 51.122; Stev. 126; Gneuss 389

(125v)   DE SANCTO IACOBO FRATRE DOMINI

1   Iacobe iuste, Iesu frater domini,
        sit tibi pia super nos conpassio,
        quos reos fecit superba iactantia
        atque fedauit mundi petulantia.

5   Annue, Christe.

Hymn 86

Use: Feastday of St. Bartholomew (August 24). See Hymn 79.
Literature: *AH* 51.122; Stev. 127; Gneuss 389

(125v)   DE SANCTO BARTHOLOMEAE

1   Bartholomeus, cæli sidus aureum,
        milies supra solis iubar radians,
        erige mentes nostras polo turbidas
        egrasque nostras sana conscientias.

5   Annue, Christe, sęculorum domine.

85/ 5   See Hymn 82.5 n.
86/ 5   See Hymn 82.5 n.

Hymn 87

Use: Feastday of St. Matthew (September 21). See Hymn 79.
Literature: *AH* 51.122; Stev. 127; Gneuss 389

(125v) DE SANCTO MATHEAE

1 Mathee sancte, bino pollens munere,
   sedulis Iesum interpella questibus,
   ut nos <in> mundi gubernet turbinibus,
   ne post æternus sorbeat interitus.

5 Annue, Christe.

Hymn 88

Use: Feastday of St. Philip (May 1, but since 1955 celebrated on May
    11). See Hymn 79.
Literature: *AH* 51.122; Stev. 127; Gneuss 390

(125v) DE SANCTO PHILIPPO

1 Proni rogamus, Philippe,/ os lampadis,
   pias cęlestis aures pulsa iudicis,
   ut que meremur repellat supplicia
   et quę precamur det superna gaudia.

5 Annue, Christe, seculorum domine.

87/ 1 *bino ... munere:* possibly a reference to the fact that Matthew
       was both an apostle and an evangelist
    4 *sorbeat:* sc. *nos*
    5 See Hymn 82.5 n.
88/ 1 *os lampadis:* this is the Hebrew etymology of Philip's name; see
       Isidore of Seville, *Etymologiae* VIII.9.16.
    5 See Hymn 82.5 n.

Hymn 89

Use: Feastday of Sts. Simon and Jude Taddeus (October 28). See Hymn 79.
Literature: *AH* 51.122; Stev. 128; Gneuss 390

(125v)   DE SANCTO SIMONE ET IUDE

1   Beate Simon et Taddee inclite,
cernite nostros gemitus cum fletibus,
quique per lapsum meruimus barathrum,
per uos cęlorum mereamur aditum.

5   Annue, Christe, seculorum domine.

Hymn 90

Use: Feastday of St. Thomas (December 21). See Hymn 79.
Literature: *AH* 51.122; Stev. 128; Gneuss 390

(125v)   DE SANCTO THOMA

1   O Thoma, Christi perlustrator lateris,
per illa sancta te rogamus uulnera,
quę mundi cuncta deluerunt crimina,
nostros reatus terge tuis precibus.

5   Annue, Christe.

89/ rubric The feasts of these two saints are probably celebrated together because in all the lists of the apostles that can be found in the Gos-
pels (e.g. Mt. 10:2-4, Mc. 3:14-19) their names appear side by side.
3   *barathrum:* hell
5   See Hymn 82.5 n.
90/ 1   *Christi perlustrator lateris:* see Io. 20:27.
5   See Hymn 82.5 n.

Hymn 91

Use: Feastday of any martyr. Appointed for Nocturns in one Wi MS
(see Gneuss 68).
Literature: *AH* 51.129; Stev. 133; Gneuss 397

HYMNUS IN NATALE UNIUS MARTYRIS

1   Martyr dei, qui unicum
patris sequendo filium
uictis triumphas hostibus
uictor fruens celestibus,

5   Tui precatus munere //
126r   nostrum reatum delue
arcens mali contagium,
uitę remouens tedium.

9   Soluta sunt iam uincula
tui sacrati corporis;
nos solue uinclis sęculi
amore filii dei.

13   Deo patri sit.

Hymn 92

Use: Lauds, feastday of any martyr
Literature: *AH* 51.130; Stev. 134; Wal. 386; Gneuss 398; Szov. 65, 96

(126r)   HYMNUS AD MATUTINAM

1   Deus, tuorum militum
sors et corona, premium,

91/   rubric The 'birthday' of a martyr is his death, when he is 'born' into
heaven.
13   The doxology is that of Hymn 2.

laudes canentes martyris
absolue nexu criminis.

5   Hic nemphe mundi gaudia
et blandimenta noxia
caduca rite deputans
peruenit ad cẹlestia.

9   Poenas cucurrit fortiter
et sustulit uiriliter;
pro te refundens sanguinem
æterna dona possidet.

13   Ob hoc precatu supplici
te poscimus, piissime,
in hoc triumpho martyris
dimitte noxam seruulis.

17   Laus et perennis gloria/
deo patri et filio
sancto simul paraclyto
in sæculorum sæcula.
Amen.

Hymn 93

Use: Feastday of several martyrs. Appointed for Lauds in one Wi MS
(see Gneuss 67).
Literature: *AH* 51.128; Stev. 131; Wal. 384; Gneuss 394; Szov. 214

(126r)   HYMNUS IN NATALE PLURIMORUM
MARTYRUM

1   Rex gloriose martyrum,
corona confitentium,

92/ 5   *nemphe = nempe*

> qui respuentes terrena
> perducis ad cęlestia,

5 Aurem benignam protinus
appone nostris uocibus;
trophea sacra pangimus,
ignosce quod deliquimus.

9 Tu uincis in martyribus,
parcendo confessoribus,
tu uince nostra crimina
donando indulgentiam.

13 Deo patri sit gloria.

Hymn 94

Use: Feastday of several martyrs
Author: Rabanus Maurus? See Szov. 222.
Literature: *AH* 50.204; Stev. 132; Gneuss 395; Szov. 214, 222, 226

ITEM ALIUS YMNUS

1 Sanctorum meritis inclita gaudia
pangamus, socii, gestaque fortia,
nam gliscit animus promere cantibus
uictorum genus optimum.

126v 5 Hii sunt, quos retinens // mundus inhorruit,
ipsum nam sterili flore peraridum
spreuere penitus teque secuti sunt,
rex Christe bone, cælitus.

9 Hii pro te furias atque ferocia
calcarunt hominum seuaque uerbera,

93/ 3   *terrena:* 'orig.' *terrea* is metrically better.
    13   The doxology is that of Hymn 2.
94/ 8   *cælitus:* here 'to heaven' and not, as usual (e.g. 54.2, 67.19, etc.),
        'from heaven'

cessit his lacerans fortiter ungula
nec carpsit penetralia.

13   Cæduntur gladiis more bidentium,
nec murmur resonat, nec quærimonia,
sed corde tacito mens bene conscia
conseruat patientiam.

17   Quę uox, quæ poterit lingua retexere,
quę tu martyribus munera preparas?
rubri nam fluido sanguine laureis
ditantur bene fulgidis.

21   Te, trina deitas unaque, poscimus,
ut culpas abluas, noxia subtrahas,
des pacem famulis, sit quoque gloria
per cuncta tibi sæcula.
AMEN./

Hymn 95

Use: Feastday of any confessor
Literature: *AH* 51.134; Stev. 136; Gneuss 401; Szov. 342

(126v) 1   <I>ste confessor domini sacratus,
festa plebs cuius celebrat per orbem,
hodie letus meruit secreta
scandere cæli.

5   Qui pius, prudens, humilis, pudicus,
sobrius, castus fuit et quietus,
uita dum presens uegetauit eius
corporis artus.

9   Ad sacrum cuius tumulum frequenter
membra languentum modo sanitati,

94/ 11   *cessit his:* 'yielded to them,' i.e. was powerless to harm them
95/ rubric   The first line of 126 vb, which should contain the rubric, is blank.

> quolibet morbo fuerint grauata,
> restituuntur.

13   Unde nunc noster chorus in honore
>   ipsius hymnum canit hunc libenter,
>   ut piis eius meritis iuuemur
>   omne per euum.

17   Sit salus illi, decus atque uirtus,
>   qui supra cęli residens cacumen
>   totius mundi machinam gubernat
>   trinus et unus.

Hymn 96

Use: Feastday of any confessor
Literature: *AH* 14.138; Stev. 135; Gneuss 399

ITEM ALIUS YMNUS

1   Christe, splendor gloriæ,
>   laudes referimus tibi,
>   qui profluo miraculo //
127r   sanctorum ornas atrium.

5   Qui in pace ecclesiæ
>   florentes more lilii
>   predicauerunt populo,
>   ut replerent paradysum,

9   Sumentes arma bellica
>   contra hostis nequitiam,
>   scutum fidei, gladium
>   spiritus, pugnant fortiter.

13   In quorum ore deus est,
>   in quorum corde Christus est,

96/ 6   See Ec. 39:19.
>   9-12   See Eph. 6:16-17.

in quorum mente pietas,
iustitia, et ueritas.

17   Orti de fece pulueris
pro bonis suis meritis
similes facti angelis
fruuntur claris gaudiis.

21   Ad quorum ossa mortua
ad magnam Christi gloriam
noua crescunt miracula
dantes plebi suffragia,

25   Dum datur salus languidis,
redditur uita mortuis,
lumen refunditur cecis,
capiunt gressum debiles./

29   Te nunc oramus, domine,
eorum nos munimine
ab omni malo protege
et uitam nobis tribue.

Hymn 97

Use: Feastday of any confessor. Appointed for Lauds in one Wi MS
(see Gneuss 68).
Literature: *AH* 51.133; Stev. 137; Wal. 387; Gneuss 402

(127r)   ITEM ALIUS YMNUS

1   Iesu, redemptor omnium,
perpes corona presulum,
in hac die clementius
nostris faueto uocibus.

5   <T>ui sacrati nominis
confessor almus claruit,

96/ 17   MS reads *orti de fece puluere uel ris.*   24   *dantes = dantia.*

cuius celebrat annua
deuota plebs sollempnia.

9   <Q>ui rite mundi gaudia
huius caduca respuens
cum angelis celestibus
letis potitur premiis.

13   <H>uius benignus annue
nobis sequi uestigia,
huius precatu seruulis
dimitte noxam criminis.

17   <S>it tibi, Christe rex piissime,
tibi patrique gloria
cum spiritu paraclyto
et nunc et in perpetuum.
Amen.//

Hymn 98

Use: Feastday of any confessor
Literature: *AH* 2.77; Szov. 214

127v 1   Summe confessor sacer et sacerdos,
temporum metas rota torquet anni,
tempus est nobis, tibi consecratum
pangere festum.

5   Presul insignis meritisque clare,
te sacra cleri populique turba
corde prostrato pietate poscit,
uernula patrem,

9   Uota cunctorum releuans in aula
regis æterni foueas utrumque

98/ rubric The first line of 127va, which should contain the rubric, is blank.
10-11 *utrumque ordinem:* i.e. *cleri populique*

ordinem, cuius pius exstitisti
pastor in urbe.

13   Questibus cuncti referunt gementes
gesta culparum lacrimisque pandunt
pessime mentis animęque nigrę
crimina dira.

17   Dignaque poena reuocat in hora
nostra cum dira miseros perurget
pandere mundo uariante facta
celitus ira.

21   Tu procul casus prohibe / tonantes,
pelle peccata, tenua furorem;
pestis et morbus, petimus, recedat
sospite ciue.

25   Moribus cunctis moderare uitam,
confer et sudam placidamque mentem,
corda uirtutum meditentur arma
munere Christi.

29   Sancte, tu prebe quoties rogaris
profluos fructus pluuiasque largas,
credimus cuncta domino fauente
te dare posse.

33   Credimus Christum pretium laborum,
premium iustum studiis dedisse,
a quibus artus etiam solutus
morte bearis.

17-20 Translate: 'And the just punishment recalls them (*crimina dira*) in
the hour when the heavenly wrath forces us miserable ones to reveal our dreadful deeds on Doomsday (when the world perishes).'
25   Translate: 'direct our lives in all ways.'
35-6 Translate: ? 'through which (*studiis*) you are made happy in death
once you have parted from your limbs.' The use of *a* here is un-
usual, since *studia* are not living beings. *artus ... solutus* 'dissolved
in respect to your limbs' is a possible Latin construction.

37   Gloriam Christo patulo canamus
ore prestanti siue dominanti,
tanta qui pollet deitate simplex
trinus et unus.
AMEN.

Hymn 99

Use: Vespers, feastday of any holy virgin
Literature: *AH* 51.137; Stev. 139; Gneuss 403; Szov. 214, 341

HYMNUS DE UIRGINIBUS

1   Uirginis proles opifexque matris,
uirgo quem gessit peperitque uirgo,
uirginis festum canimus tropheum:
accipe uotum.//

128r 5   Hæc tua uirgo, duplici beata
sorte, dum gessit fragilem domare
corporis sexum, domuit cruentum
corpore seclum.

9   Inde nec mortem nec amica mortis
seua poenarum genera pauescens
sanguine fuso meruit secreta
scandere celi.

13   Huius obtentu, deus alme, nostris
parce iam culpis uitia remittens,
quo tibi puri resonemus almum
pectoris ymnum.

17   Gloria patri geniteque proli
et tibi, compar utriusque semper
spiritus alme, deus unus omni
tempore secli.
AMEN.

99/ 5   *Hæc tua uirgo:* refers not to the Virgin Mary, but to the virgin

Hymn 100

Use: Nocturns, feastday of any holy virgin
Author: Ambrose
Literature: *AH* 50.20; Stev. 140; Wal. 112; Gneuss 404; Szov. 51, 214

(128r)   HYMNUS AD NOCTURNAM

1   Iesu, corona uirginum,
          quem mater illa concepit,
          que sola uirgo parturit,
          hæc uota clemens accipe,

5   <Q>ui pascis inter lilia,
          septus choreis uirginum,
          sponsas decorans gloria
          sponsisque reddens premia;/

9   Quocumque pergis, uirgines
          secuntur atque laudibus
          post te canentes cursitant
          hymnosque dulces personant.

13   Te deprecamur, largius
          nostris adauge mentibus
          nescire prorsus omnia
          corruptionis uulnera.

17   Deo patri sit gloria.

99/   whose feast is celebrated.
100/ 2   *concepit:* 'orig.' *concipit* is metrically better.
    5   *pascis:* 'you feed'; see Cant. 2:16.
    13-16   The inf. *nescire* is dependent on the imp. *adauge:* 'We beg you,
              increase in our minds [the power] not to know all the sores of
              corruption.'
    17   The doxology is that of Hymn 2.

TEXTUAL NOTES

AH = *Analecta hymnica*, *B* = BL MS. Add. 37517, *D* = Durham
Cathedral MS. B III 32, *V* = BL MS. Cotton Vespasian D XII,
Wal. = Walpole

2.9	excitatus *V:* excitato *B*
4.6	tribuat *V:* tribut *B*
5.13	abscesserit *V:* abscescerit *B*
10.8	polluantur *V:* pulluantur *B*
12.13	somnum *ed.* (sompnum *V*): somnium *B*
14.12	labascat *Wal.:* labescat *BVD*
15.14	retundat *V:* retundet *B*
15.21	Christusque *V:* Spiritusque *B*
23.11	gestit *D:* gesti *V:* gestis *B*
24 (rubric)	MATUTINAM *D:* LAUDES *V:* NOCTURNAM *B*
24.2	fatiscit *Wal.:* fatescat *VD:* fatescit *B*
34.12	bonis *V:* bons *B*
36.4	ascendit *ed.:* scandit *BVD*
36.12	ad *AH* 50.201: et *BVD*
40.12	nostris *V:* nrostris *B*
41.22	obhorruit *V (prose):* horruit *B*
42.9	personat *V:* personet *B*
43.13	petimus *supplied from V: missing in B*
43.20	unus *V:* unuus *B*
44.2	perhennis *V:* perhenni *B*
44.10	gaudentium *V:* gaudium *B*
45.11	reddentes *V:* redentes *B*
49.6	pectore *D:* pectori *BV*
50.2	horis *V:* oris *B*
50.3	occasu *Wal.:* occasum *BVD*
50.16	ludificatam *V:* ludificata *B.* polluat *V:* pulluat *B*
52.26	plasmatis *V:* plasmati *B*
52.31	quo *D:* quod *BV*
55.10	gratia *D:* gratiam *BV*
55.11	mira *V:* mire *B*

55.27	gratiam prestes *supplied from V: missing in B*
56 (rubric)	ADNUNTIATIONE *V:* PURIFICATIONE *B*
56.26	germine *V:* gerimne *B*
57.8	Eue *V:* aue *B*
64.25-6	Sit nobis cum cælestibus / commune manens gaudium *V:* Sit nobis cælestibus / cum commune manens gaudium *B*
65.21	coitur *V (prose) and as a gloss in D:* cogniti *B*
65.28	concrepat *V:* concrepet *B*
67.12	quos *V:* quo *B*
67.25	laus *V:* lus *B*
69.3	polluti *V:* pulluti *B*
69.27	auferentem *V:* auferenten *B*
72.20	splendet *V:* splendet *B*
74.11	ad istud *V:* et istum *B*
76.15	uestris orationibus *supplied from V: missing in B*
77.6	adornent *V:* adornant *B*
78.1	confessor *V:* consessor *B*
78.8	reformas *ed.:* reformans *BD*
79.3	apostolorum gloriam *D:* apostolum gloria *B*
79.16	reddentes *V:* redentes *B*
80.30	ut *V:* et *B*
81.8	soluantur *D:* saluantur *B*
81.13	Dole *V:* doli *B*
82.4	euacuato *in conformity with Hymn 70.16:* euacuata *B*
86.2	milies *V:* miles *B*
87.3	in *supplied from V: missing in B*
88.3	ut que *V:* atque *B*
90 (rubric)	THOMA *D:* THOMAE *B*
91.12	filii *V:* fili *B*
92.2	corona *V:* corora *B*
94.16	conseruat *V:* conseruet *B*
95.16	omne *V:* onne *B*
95.19	machinam *V:* machinan *B*
96.30	munimine *V:* munine *B*
97.18	tibi *V:* tib *B*
98.35	solutus *AH* 2.77: solutos *B*
99.14	remittens *V:* remttens *B*

APPENDIX

THE CREED

1 Credo in unum Deum, Patrem omnipotentem, factorem caeli et terrae,
visibilium omnium et invisibilium.
Et in unum Dominum Jesum Christum, Filium Dei unigenitum; et ex
Patre natum ante omnia saecula, Deum de Deo, lumen de lumine,
5 Deum verum de Deo vero, genitum, non factum, consubstantialem
Patri: per quem omnia facta sunt; qui propter nos homines et propter
nostram salutem descendit de caelis; et incarnatus est de Spiritu
Sancto ex Maria Virgine et homo factus est; crucifixus etiam pro
nobis, sub Pontio Pilato passus et sepultus est. Et resurrexit tertia die,
10 secundum Scripturas, et ascendit in caelum: sedet ad dexteram Patris.
Et iterum venturus est cum gloria judicare vivos et mortuos: cujus
regni non erit finis.
Et in Spiritum Sanctum, Dominum et vivificantem, qui ex Patre Filioque
procedit; qui cum Patre et Filio simul adoratur et conglorificatur: qui
15 locutus est per Prophetas.
Et unam sanctam catholicam et apostolicam Ecclesiam.
Confiteor unum baptisma in remissionem peccatorum, et exspecto
resurrectionem mortuorum, et vitam venturi saeculi. Amen.

ALPHABETICAL LIST OF FIRST LINES

(References are to hymn numbers, not to pages.)